LEAP OF FAITH 3

The Packer Hall of Faith

Steve and his angel Kim.

Kim,

*I know I don't tell you nearly enough just
what you mean to me. I cherish you, not
because of the extraordinary things you
can do or what you have been through,
but because you're you.*

I love you.

xox

Steve

LEAP OF FAITH 3

The Packer Hall of Faith

Steve Rose

WINNERS SUCCESS NETWORK PUBLISHING
Neenah, Wisconsin

Leap of Faith 3: The Packer Hall of Faith
First edition, first printing
Copyright ©1998 by Steve Rose

ISBN: 0-9666-819-0-8

Sequel to: Leap of Faith: God Must Be a Packer Fan 1996
            Leap of Faith 2: God Loves Packer Fans 1997

For information or manuscript submission guidelines,
address inquiries to:

Winners Success Network Publishing
Post Office Box 404
Neenah, WI 54957-0404
e.mail   leap@lofrose.com

Publisher.................Steve Rose
Editor......................Kathi Pollard

All Scripture quotations are taken from the
King James Version of the Bible.

Cover Design and manuscript setup by Mike Utech
Graphic Design by Jill VanderLoop
Printed in the United States of America
Cover photograph courtesy of Vernon Biever
Hall of Faith photographs courtesy of the Green Bay Packers

CONTENTS

CONTENTS CONT.

ACKNOWLEDGMENTS

I thank my Lord and Savior, Jesus Christ, for giving me the opportunity to serve Him. I praise Him for all He is doing.

To my family, you're still the greatest. We aren't the Cleavers, but I don't think we're doing too badly.

Thanks to my Pastor and friend, Steve Nickel, of my home church Fox Valley Christian Fellowship in Kimberly, WI. You and your flock are so awesome.

Here's a tribute to two men who are very much responsible for this book, Ken Ruettgers and John Michels. They let me into their world so that I could get all that God wanted me to get to put in here.

My hat goes off once more to my right hand men, Mike Utech and Bob Gardinier. A man could not find two *truer* friends. Your counsel, help and endless sacrifice has brought us to where we are today. Where are we anyway? Seriously, you guys are so much fun to work with.

To Kathi Pollard, my editor, who God brought to this party just in the nick of time. Thanks for allowing God to mold you into the person you are. You are the most obedient servant I have ever known. After saying that, I hope you will let up on your relentless teasing of me!

Thanks to Arni Jacobson for his contribution to this work. God's hand is in what you are doing "big time," Pastor.

To my faithful friend, Brad Vivoda, thanks for putting up with me

"The Two From USC and Me." Steve with friends and radio co-hosts Ken Ruettgers (L) and John Michels. (R)

on the road and the hundreds of miles in rain and snow.

Thanks to Bob Harlen, Lee Remmel, Paula Martin and Linda McCrossin of the Packers. You're so nice.

And with love, I thank Nathan and Jenny Pollard and Tanya DeVoe. I didn't get to know you while you were on this side of heaven, but someday I will. What your untimely departures have meant to my ministry is inexplicable.

Foreword

By John Michels

John Michels, the Packers #1 draft pick in 1996 and Steve Rose

It is round three for Steve Rose. It is perhaps the most important round of them all. Does God still love the Packers? It is a question that many have pondered since that dreaded night in San Diego.

Steve has developed a relationship with the Packers that gives him a special perspective of what really goes on behind the scenes at Lambeau Field as well as what's happening in the personal lives of the men who wear the green and gold. Steve and I became friends two years ago and realized that we share a common perspective for ministry to the Green Bay community. We both want to show the Packers as regular people, and show how Christ can use regular people to impact lives.

It used to be a joke in college that I would end up playing pro football in Green Bay, Wisconsin. As a boy who grew up in San Diego and who played college ball at the University of Southern California, my idea of hell freezing over was Green Bay. It was the coldest place my friends and I could imagine, and they always teased me that that's where I would end up.

When the phone rang on April 20, 1996, that joke became reality. The Green Bay Packers had just made me there number-one pick in the draft. When I arrived in Green Bay, I realized that the mental picture I had carried around for so long was completely false. In fact, Green Bay was the furthest thing from hell that I had seen.

From the football perspective, there is a love affair between this community and its football team which is unlike any that exists in professional athletics. To see ten thousand people lining the fence of the practice field on a Wednesday afternoon in August was proof enough to me that I was in for a very special experience.

From a personal perspective, as I began to build relationships with my teammates, I began to see another reason why this place was far from being hell. Christians were everywhere - Keith Jackson, Don Beebe, Ken Ruettgers, Reggie White, Eugene Robinson, Adam Timmerman, to name a few. I had never been a part of a team that had so many men openly and actively proclaiming their love for Jesus Christ.

Ken Ruettgers was recovering from knee surgery in 1996 when he asked me if I would like to take his place as co-host of the radio show "Timeout" on Q90 F.M. Steve and I hit it off. We saw a community with such a passionate love for their football team. Our vision was, and is, for this community to have that same passion for Jesus Christ.

Steve has been able to reveal the Packers as human beings, not idols to be worshiped. Through the radio program and his books he has shown the public that the Green Bay Packers are not gods, merely men. He has challenged the public to evaluate why they adore these men. Is it because of who they are, or simply what they do?

I have signed a lot of autographs since I have been here, and I have had people tell me that I was a "good guy" for doing so. It made me evaluate why they thought I was a good guy. Was it because of who I am, or simply because I had done what they had asked me to do? Did those people really know whether or not I was a "good guy?"

Steve has used this ministry to show that good guys are not those who sign autographs or perform well on Sundays. Good guys are those who walk in integrity, love their families and, most importantly, love the Lord.

What "good guys" do you and your family look up to? Do you know if they really are good guys? Upon what do you base your reasoning?

When I read Steve's first book, I began to see God's plan unfolding for this community. God had brought a group of men together through whom He was going to touch thousands of lives. The groundwork had been done. I could sense, through reading <u>Leap of Faith</u>, that God was doing something incredible in this town. Leap 2 revealed just what that incredible work was. Steve has always said that it is amazing what people can accomplish when nobody cares who gets the credit. Well, God brought a group of football players together who wanted to give God all the credit, and He lead them to a World Championship.

The impact that Super Bowl XXXI had on this community, and the nation, was tremendous. Everyone knew that this team was special, but to hear and read that God was the reason for our success showed a perspective that few teams in history have shown.

With Super Bowl XXXII behind us, and that devastating loss to the Denver Broncos still fresh on everyone's minds, people are wondering whether God is still a Packer fan. In <u>Leap of Faith 3</u> with a style that only Steve Rose possesses, we will see that it was in defeat, perhaps more than in victory, that God revealed His greatness through the Green Bay Packers.

Steve is more than just a writer about professional football players. He has built relationships with several athletes. His writing reveals something that most authors about professional sports miss; these men, who so many worship and adore, are just regular people. They have pains, struggles, insecurities and problems, just like anyone else. Steve shows the Green Bay Packers as they really are, just ordinary people like you. In a real and personal way, Steve describes the miracles that God has worked in and through the lives of these football players. Come and discover what God can do in your life as you read about what He has done in the lives of the men who wear the green and gold.

Ken Ruettgers once told me that a man came up to him and shared how great he thought it was that we prayed on the fifty-yard line after every game. Ken stopped for a moment, then responded by asking the man, "Where is *your* fifty-yard line?"

I want to encourage each reader of this book to find his/her fifty-yard line, whether it be in the office or in the home. Be amazed at what can be accomplished when God gets all the credit!

Sit back. Enjoy this book. Decide for yourself whether or not God is still a Packer fan.

INTRODUCTION

One More Leap of Faith

I'm glad nobody told me. I'm glad I didn't find out till after the first book was out how tough it is to get a book published. Experts in the literary field will confirm that a "nobody," especially a first-time author, shouldn't have been able to do it. But with God's anointing, his "super" on my "natural," here is Leap of Faith 3 of the series.

What I'm trying to say is it appears this book, like its older brother and sister Leap of Faith:God Must Be A Packer Fan and Leap of Faith 2:God Loves Packer Fans, is a miracle baby. None of them should have made it past conception much less have been born. But when God gives you a word to get out, He'll use whoever He wants. In this case, it's me.

If there is one man, under God here on earth, who is responsible for making this trilogy possible it's former Packer Ken Ruettgers. Old number 75's vision for a Christian radio program, which began in 1994 on Q-90 in Green Bay, blossomed into what is now the "Leap of Faith Sports Radio Show." (It's currently heard on 25 radio stations and 33 different frequencies throughout the Midwest.) Ken and I co-hosted it through the 1995 season.

Unlike the books, the show never needed to beat the odds. Anything with a Packer platform in Wisconsin flies. But, the Leap of Faith books, well, the odds I guess should have been stacked against it.

I like what Pepper Burruss, the trainer of the Packers, said on a show last year explaining how Ken Ruettgers had rebounded from his back injury in 1995. Odds said Ken was going to miss about eight games. Pepper said "Ken Ruettgers knew odds are for losers." What he was trying to say is that true champions work hard to achieve. While many others hope they can make it, the one who does succeed has a well-calculated plan fueled with faith and enthusiasm.

I guess sales consultant Pam Lontos said it best in her 1986 book, "Don't Tell Me It Can't Be Done Till I've Already Done It." It's pertinent here. I'm no fool. If I'd have known that the manuscript would have had any chance of not becoming a book, there is no way this insecure person would have even taken the chance.

Let me review to show you how this series has progressed. After five months of pounding the key pad, (from December of 1995 to April 1996) about 40,000 words were sent off to be combed, massaged and otherwise edited. From there it was whisked to the printer where it seemed like an eternity till September 1, 1996, when the first copy was made available for sale in Tampa, Florida. Ironically, nearly 40,000 have been sold of Leap 1, which is about a book a word. (Maybe I should shoot for about a half-a-million words for this one!)

The hot, muggy, rainy day of the very first book signing is emblazoned on my memory forever. Sitting to my left was a Packer legend I'd met as a little boy and had admired dearly. But these days I really have come to appreciate him. Matter of fact, as of late, this man's testimony and how it relates to impacting people in Wisconsin is the most impressive that I have ever heard in Packer history. More on the "mystery man" later. (If you read Leap 2 you know who we're talking about, but you have to hear the update later.)

As you know, I've been in on many of the great stories the last few years with the Packers. The unique relationships which have developed from appearances, book signings, radio and now TV shows have given me scores of memories of and experiences with some of the finest men ever to come through the locker room at 1265 Lombardi in Green Bay.

In Leap 1 and Leap 2, we did the best we could to reveal the real people behind the facemasks of the Packer helmets, to expose their hearts, homes and lives. We praise God that your cards, calls and letters confirmed that's what you wanted. Leap 2 attempted more of an in-depth inquiry into whether we're worshipping football players in Green Bay rather than God. "Are the Super Bowls going to matter to any of us in a hundred years?" and other such questions were addressed.

In this compilation, bringing to completion the trilogy, we'll try one more time to take you where few have been able to go. I also have resurrected a few of the guys whose walk with the Lord Jesus Christ has never been chronicled until now - men whose faith was prominent, but was never made an issue till today. To put a cap on the project, we'll be inducting a few of these role models into the Green Bay Packer Hall of Faith.

From Carroll Dale of the Lombardi days to a few of Holmgren's heroes today, many of these warriors will tell you just the way they see it. You'll hear of their faith, values and standards. It's a perspective the mainstream media has not spent a lot of time pursuing for reasons for which they will have to give account.

In writing the foreword for Leap 2, my friend and marriage mentor Kenny Ruettgers said that you'd get a perspective like none other. I hope you are among the thousands of folks who have found this to be the case. Because of the "safe" environment that the radio and TV shows offer, the guys have felt free to talk about some things they may not have elsewhere to the media.

I only need go as far back as week three of the 1997 "Leap of Faith Sports Radio Show" when, along the network lines with "my rock" and co-host John Michels, Don Beebe appeared with teammates Robert Brooks and Eugene Robinson. Some of the most powerful dialogue occurred there.

Deep into that classic program, Beebe told a story of his friend, Jeff, that may make the hair on the back of your neck stand up. It was bold...really bold. It had substance to it. I'll share it in upcoming pages. Without reservation I can say it is one of the most astounding stories I have ever heard...bar none. I can promise that this testimony may change someone's life eternally! (Perhaps yours!)

If this book *only* contained some of the precious Godly dialogue from the Leap of Faith Sports Radio Shows, which it does, it would be worth reading. If it were the only thing included, it would be pure gold. I've come to realize that it would be a tragedy (and an act of pure selfishness on my part) not to share the profound statements of faith, values and inside stories that the guys have shared with me which they want people to know.

It just so happens that we have about 22 hours on tape. We won't share all of it, but certainly the highlights. It has taken about twenty-five hours alone just to listen to the tapes which we have selected to print in this book. They were worth every minute in anticipation of the joy, hope, help and encouragement they will bring you. At the end of this book, we let you know how you can order these rare gems, too.

What I've learned is this: the guys have been looking for some time for a place where they can freely share their feelings, without censorship, editing or restriction. Because the Lord is the Executive Producer of The Leap of Faith Sports Radio Show, players have been given the latitude that otherwise may not have been available on many of the other Packer shows.

In large part because of the trust the guys felt while sharing since the inception of the show in 1994, they have been willing to "lay it on the line." It continues even today with John Michels and me. We also have the "Leap of Faith TV Show." (Details of where you can see it are also in the pages ahead.)

The key message that will be stressed during these pages is that a good number of the Green Bay Packers are not exclusively about football. It's their job, the vehicle and platform from which they speak. Going back to 1995, I heard statements from players like, "We just want to win so we can widen our platform on which to be good role models" or "We just wanna win a Super Bowl so we can reach more people with the words of the saving grace of Jesus Christ!" It may come as a surprise, but these words were echoed by many other players from the "glory day" years also.

Friend, it's become apparent that the message of salvation offered through Jesus Christ, proclaimed by many Packer players over the years, has many times been lost in the shuffle. Can you recall a headline in your local paper that acknowledged the faith of any one player? Do you recall an interview where any of the guys were able to share the gospel or to proclaim that nothing will matter a hundred years from now outside of their relationships with Jesus Christ?

An argument may be made that there are certain places which are saved for this type of material. Perhaps so, but I know that this book is one of those places. Like the other books, if the message that Jesus Christ is the reason for the faith on this team offends you, then so be it. I won't take it personally. I'm not the message, just the messenger.

Will you take one more leap of faith and really pray that the content of this book can find you? I mean really FIND you. That's the purpose of the first two books and this one as well. So what's in this for you? Well, if it has eternal rewards for you, wouldn't that be plenty?

Open your heart to God's words here, please. It can be the greatest thing to ever happen to you. If you want to receive it, say these words, "Lord, I pray to receive your message of truth that will set me free, Amen."

Ahead, you'll learn about a young man who says that Christ is the One who helps him handle a job that comes with loads of pressure. From Bend, Oregon, his chances of playing for the Green Bay Packers should have been nil last year. But God had other plans. He'll recount how his life literally changed in a split second in the autumn of 1997 after a little bit of a "fall." You'll be able to relate.

I will share who continues to be the most huggable and lovable of the whole green and gold bunch. Also, I'll tell you who my all-time favorite guy is in my opportunities of ministry with the Pack. I've been asked this question a thousand times, and I had promised I'd keep neutral on the subject, but I'm going to answer it in this book!

Who bought a bike for a neighbor boy? What player's testimony impacted me the most during 1997? And I'll tell you what Packer the Lord prompted me to call, weeping, to tell him how deeply his ministry and family have touched me? Because of Leap 1, what former Packer released a book after the Super Bowl? And...I received a "sentence sermon" from one of the fellas on May 29, 1998, that riveted my soul. What did he say, why and who is he? The "Lambeau Leaper," Robert Brooks, reveals more unbelievable insight into his miraculous recovery and how the Lord walked him through it.

Like Leap 2, we'll take you with us on a few dates of the Leap of Faith "Temporary Insanity" Book Tour, too.

There are a couple real treats for me in this project that I know will bless you also. Specifically, I'm referring to the participation of two very special people.

One is Kathi Pollard. I can safely say that had not God provided her to edit this book, I wouldn't have been comfortable doing it right now. Her arrival for Leap 3 taught me that God is "seldom early and never late." Her talent, touch and tenderness hold this series of ideas together. More than a great editor, she's an even better person, and a precious sister in Christ.

Reverend Arni Jacobson, Senior Pastor of Bayside Christian Fellowship in Green Bay, is the other blessing this time around. His gift to us entitled, "The Last Chapter of #66," is far more than that. Much more. Over the years this man of God has mentored many of the Christians on the team.

Pastor Jacobson will tell all of us what's really important and, specifically, ask us the only question in life that matters. More importantly, he has the answer. He's not the answer, but he'll share the One who is. Pastor will pass along some insights into the "Packer platform" from his view that are just extraordinary. I trust that you, too, will agree it will bring a proper end to this divinely inspired trilogy. And it's all only one more leap of faith away.

CHAPTER 1

Is San Diego Silence Golden?

I couldn't believe what was about to occur. Before the game I had convinced myself that it wouldn't be the worst thing in the world if it happened. I was realizing in this moment that I really didn't mean it. I am referring to whether the Packers were to somehow lose to the Denver Broncos in Super Bowl XXXII. Sure, I'd thought about the possibility and even mentioned it during the "Leap of Faith Sports Radio Show." Now I was about to learn that it's easy to "talk the talk," but "walking the walk" might be a whole other story.

Brett Favre was walking off the field after a botched fourth-down play staring at the scoreboard and time clock in Qualcomm Stadium in San Diego. He looked like the most surprised person on the planet. I was a close second. The Broncos were going to do a couple of those sickening "kneel down" things and then start the party. They did just that.

How could this be possible? The so-called experts had the Packers as nearly two touchdown favorites! Besides, the NFC always wins this game. What was going on here? The San Diego silence I felt for ten minutes wasn't golden. Matter of fact, it was a rather penetrating, sickening feeling. I was asking myself, "God, why did we lose?" The fact that we played so poorly wasn't good enough for me.

Really, if anybody could ask the question, "God, what are you doing?"

it could be me, right? I had it all figured out. After all, God really could get a lot of glory by allowing the Packers to prevail once again. It wasn't to be. Though God has entrusted me with a powerful and unique Packer ministry, and has shared with me why He has chosen to use this team for His glory, it was also apparent to me that He owed me no explanation.

Even brief analysis says that He doesn't owe any of us one. Did you want one then, too? Do you still want one? For me the loss brought two questions to mind. The first is, "What did the armchair quarterbacks and experts see during the game?"

The VCR replay showed the Packers, despite repeated denials in the post-game interviews, looked a tad flat and lackluster. Brett Favre gave the Packers an early lead with a touchdown pass to Antonio Freeman. From there the champs became entwined in the battle of their lives. Along the way the Broncos spotted a weakness. As Todd Korth of the Packer Report said they "went after it faster than a Cheesehead for the last brat on the grill."

The weakness was the Packer defensive line and the weapon to attack it was running back Terrell Davis. His patented cutback moves off of the "toss sweep" racked up 157 yards. And as former Packer and Green Bay TV Sportscaster Larry McCarren said, "If he hadn't gotten a migraine in the second quarter, (which kept him out) the statisticians may have needed a slide rule to count his yardage." By the finish Davis had given his headache to the former Super Bowl champions.

As much as the loss stung, even Reggie gave the credit where credit was due. "He (Davis) did a good job of picking his holes. We didn't do a good enough job of getting upfield and getting to him." Reggie also took his hat off to John Elway who had fallen short in previous appearances.

So, that's what people saw and and that's what people said.

The second question is, "What did God see?" Do you suppose He had to watch the films? Do you think God was watching the game or did He have other, more important, things to do? My guess is He had to turn on "His boys" (those Packers) cause, after all, God is a Packer fan, right? Somebody insinuated that somewhere. I think it was in a book. (Wonder what the bum is doing now?) Actually, I'll talk about whether God is still a Packer fan in the pages ahead.

Just like many of the other thoughts in these books, I believe through faith I have heard from God on the issue. Here's what I feel He saw in Super Bowl XXXII. He saw an opportunity to show the power of His

Word making many verses in His book come alive. Here's just a couple of examples. Just as summer precedes autumn, "pride comes before a fall" (Prov. 16:18). There is some evidence to suggest that the Packers may have been just a bit overconfident.

One Packer player told me two days after the game, "Steve, let me assure you that what happened in San Diego was suppose to happen." He went as far as to say he was really happy for Terrell Davis, the game MVP and San Diego native, who'd had his number retired that week at his high school. Pretty cool, huh? Have you softened for those lovable Broncos yet?

One of the Packer participants of the first two Super Bowls had some ideas of what may have happened against the Broncos. When I chatted with him about it he said, "Maybe we underestimated the Broncos, but even more probable is that the Packers may have overestimated themselves." Pretty strong statement. And can you imagine how tough it may have been for a former Packer to say it?

I guess we could possibly include the above statement as evidence to Scripture that the "exalted will be humbled and the humbled will be exalted" (1 Pet. 5:6). A great example of the humbled being exalted was Denver coach Mike Shanahan. After the game, it was revealed that he had told his players to not say anything to put gas on the Packer fire, but rather to show tons of respect. This was especially tough for the outspoken Shannon Sharpe, the All-Pro tight end for the Broncos, but he managed.

Sure enough, after further review, the Broncos could be heard saying things like, "Oh, those Packers are soooooo good....and we're gonna have to play a perfect game to beat them." They sounded like they were as scared as turkeys the day before Thanksgiving. It was a great act which worked wonderfully.

Meanwhile, on the other side, our buddies were picking up the USA today to check the 13-point spread. They listened as the Summeralls, Maddens and Costases claimed all the team had to do was show up. Packer players, I'm sure, also opened their ears to the experts talking about how the green and gold had simply "too much firepower for the Broncos to handle." Why didn't somebody tell the Broncos? The fact the Packers were too good for Denver was true---except for three hours on January 25, 1997.

Did you see any of the Packer interviews after the game? Poor

Derrick Mayes was interviewed outside the locker room after hitting the shower. He looked like he had just been hit by a locomotive. I don't think he had given much thought to the possibility of defeat. He wasn't alone.

As a story goes, one of the guys sat in his hotel room staring at the wall all night. There was a party going on, but he really didn't feel like putting his tux and patent leather shoes on. To make matters worse, the guy's girlfriend broke up with him that night. Wow, that wasn't his day. Losing the Super Bowl and a girlfriend. Isn't God cruel? Of course not.

God knows us better than we know ourselves and He allows things that align with His kingdom purposes. Could it be that God had determined that He could get more glory by allowing a Packer loss than a win? Is it that simple? Can we throw out the statistics, commentary and the analysis and trust God's designs and intentions?

As we've claimed in this trilogy, God is only interested in one thing-- the state of your spirit, period. He's got the "big picture" in mind. Do you suppose He sees a Packer in grief and grieves as well? The tragedy is not in the loss, but the fact they'd grieve over such a trivial matter in the first place.

So what's the answer? It's to simply trust and obey. To know God is to love Him. To love Him is to obey Him. To obey Him is to trust Him. To trust Him is to let go of trusting in our own understanding, which is difficult to do. It's impossible without His help.

To some fans in Green Bay, and throughout the country, the green and gold went about their business entering the contest as the Super Bowl XXXI Champs and by early evening on January 25 were Super Bowl XXXII chumps. Not to God. He's got a plan. So is He still a Packer fan? We'll take a look at that next. It's the turn of a page and yet another leap of faith away.

CHAPTER 2

The "Leap of Faith Sports Radio Show"

T he beginning of the 1997 season brought with it a new beginning for our unique Christian Packer radio ministry. Birthed as the "Timeout" radio program in 1994, this gift from the men from the walls and halls of the Packer Hall of Faith to the community has now become the "Leap of Faith Sports Radio Show."

It all premiered in 1994. Ken Ruettgers and I would brave the cold early mornings to sip hot coffee, eat doughnuts and get ready for the 7 a.m. live program which aired on Q-90 in the Green Bay market. Then, in 1995, Ken and I moved to Mondays at 6 p.m. When Ken retired, John Michels and Don Beebe shared the platform and brought a unique sound to the airwaves. It has since moved forward with a couple of changes.

Along with the fresh handle, the program is now shared with some 25 radio affiliates on 33 frequencies over the Midwest. John Michels has been a superb co-host and sidekick. We have developed a tremendous respect for and friendship with one another in the process. To top it all off, we now host the "Leap of Faith TV Show" which can be seen over parts of Wisconsin. (For a schedule of TV and radio stations call (920) 995-2395.)

All the recent growth to network the program was not without sweat, belief and growing pains, however. The guy who dove into the trenches to make this happen in 1997 was Bob Gardinier. He is the Executive Director of my Winners Success Radio Network. Bob is one of the nicest people you'll ever meet. He's loaded with a smooth voice and great people skills. Bob is a brother in the Lord and, most importantly to me, one of my closest friends.

I guess no one told Bob that you're supposed to need a bunch of "glossy press kits and demo tapes" to call and sell the show to the stations. Bob sold twenty five radio affiliates on the program in a month! From the remarkable success they experienced carrying the show, they're very happy that he did. Now, because of the show and the books, there's a TV show. For all of these blessings we give Christ the glory. It borders on the miraculous.

By July (before the '97 campaign) I got in touch with John Michels who agreed joyfully to co-host the show for the second season in a row. The previous year I'd worked with both Don Beebe and John. Michels is not only a good football player, he is a non-compromising man of Christ who saw this as a great platform to share his faith. And that he did.

Our ministry quickly went to a whole new level of intensity, trust and sparkle as the radio season began. You'll witness this as you're brought into the studio over the next pages. This big man never shied away from any of the tough questions as he personally experienced not only one of the toughest years in his career, but in his life. You'll see that at only 24, John's walk with the Lord is well beyond those years. His maturity, honesty, intelligence and flat out adoration for Jesus is obvious.

It didn't take long to record and air along the network what I believe could be the greatest Packer sports-related programming ever aired in history. I don't say that loosely, but because I mean it. For instance, four Packers converged on the recording studio on September 8, 1997. It was a memorable day shortly after a Packer loss to the Eagles. It aired the following weekend. You'll experience it in just a moment.

Shortly after, a starry-eyed rookie from Iowa named Ross Verba came in and talked about how excited he was to be on the program. This celebrity stuff was really new to him. Then we became acquainted with Paul Frase who may go down as a guy with the greatest story to which those who have family burdens can relate.

Weeks passed and we met Doug Pederson, Ryan Longwell and the other regulars, people like Pepper Burruss, Chaplain Steve Newman,

Reggie and Robert. Ken even came in which was an emotional high for me. It was real and it was fun. It was real fun!

Reverend Kevin Penniman from Gentle Shepherd Church in Rockford, Illinois, a pilot and my friend, made a couple of appearances and shared God's wisdom, too. Other guests about whom you read (in Leap 2) dropped by. Paul McKellips who wrote "Reggie's Prayer" (the movie starring White) stopped in for the first show. Then John Gillespie from the Rawhide Chapters had some more great Packer/Rawhide Ranch stories.

One thing I am cautious in mentioning here is that some of the most precious moments ever spent with the guys are when the microphones are off... the clowning around, the teasing between us, and the daily stuff during the breaks that they may feel is a bit too personal to share. I hesitate to say this because it's rude to touch on something and then not to share it. But, I hope you understand.

One such moment, however, had us roaring at the halfway point during a break in the show with Reggie. He was giving a somewhat wild version of the truth as to why Christ was crucified. He brought a whole new light to it that was somewhat bizarre yet so astoundingly true, we laughed. Now, let me make myself clear. There is nothing humorous about our Lord and Savior's crucifixion. Read on, and judge for yourself.

I asked White to share it during the show and he did. You'll hear it in the second half. The Minister of the Defense told a forthright version of what the "locals" who had put Christ on the cross were thinking. What reasons (besides the obvious) helped to lead up to the tragedy at Calvary? You'll invariably find yourself sharing it with others in the church and community.

As I touched on earlier in the book, if the transcripts of the shows to follow were all that was included here, I believe it would be a complete book. I hear the lines, the laughter and the wisdom in my mind over and over. As I hear the tapes, I can feel John and I bonding. I fall deeper in admiration of Robert Brooks. I realize why Don Beebe was chosen by the Lord and so much more. Your feeling will be exclusively yours and speak to you in a powerful way.

I believe the words you'll read that we've written and the shows we heard are God guided and inspired. I know that they will impact you greatly for a long time. You'll enjoy spending time with a group of people who play football as the "front" used to share their faith in Christ. These same ones are being inducted to spend eternity in the Green Bay Packer Hall-of-Faith.

So now, close your eyes. Enter the studio. Welcome to the "1997 Leap of Faith Sports Radio Show Zone." Relax. Laugh and cry with us. Bob Gardinier has set a chair for you right next to me. And I see John has brought you an extra doughnut and a cup of coffee. Best of all, it's only a leap of faith away.

CHAPTER 3

The Leap of Faith
Sports Radio Show 97'

Week #3 • "The Gang"

Show # 9703 (Recorded Sept. 8, 1997)

Aired on WSRN stations September 12-14, 1997

Steve Rose and John Michels, co-hosts
Don Beebe, Robert Brooks, Eugene Robinson, guests

John Michels ambled his way into the private studios tucked cozily downstairs in the building where we record which is within ear and eye shot of Lambeau Field. As he passed through the doorway I looked up into the eyes of the second- year tackle. We exchanged a handshake and pleasantries and then I got down to business.

"Whose coming in, big man?" I questioned.

"Robert, Don and Eugene," he said coolly. "They want to help you with the release of Leap 2," he finished as he plopped himself down.

"You're kiddin!"

"They'll be here," he said slamming his Pepsi.

I'd kept in contact with Brooks and he certainly hadn't leaked anything to me about coming in. I'd only known Eugene in passing. Don and I had worked together the year before. I'd caught Robinson in glancing and was pumped to have the chance to have him on the show.

It quickly ran through my head that you just don't get Robert Brooks, Don Beebe and Eugene Robinson on any program or appearance docket--anywhere. But today was different. God had predestined this hour for the ages.

Sure enough, within a couple of minutes of John's profession, I peaked out the door and walking down the stairs were Don Beebe and Robert Brooks! With the bounce of a sixth grader I hopped off my chair to greet them. I walked out the doorway of the room as they approached.

"Don, how you doing buddy?"

"Good, Steve."

"Robert," I said excitedly as I shook his paw while wrapping my left hand around his skinny waste. "It's great to see you, brother!" We kept walking toward the studio.

"How's it going, Steve?" inquired the walking miracle who'd survived his devastating knee injury from 1996. I couldn't resist telling him the great news. "Our next book is out in a couple of days!"

"That's what I heard," Brooks commented.

Sure enough, just as Michels had promised, a few moments after Beebe and Brooks came the arrival of Eugene Robinson who, as usual, was glowing like a lamp.

Poor Bob Gardinier. While we all laughed and chatted, he was getting situated to engineer the recording. This was his first year with me and his actions reminded me of the day I met Ken Ruettgers and Sterling Sharpe years before. You know, today it's easy for me to say, "They're just people." But, truth be told, the first time you meet these guys you are star-struck. It's probably just as well he hadn't had any warning.

Bob was fidgeting with the recording equipment as I introduced him to "The Gang." Another guest with us was Christine Winkelmen, Packerwomaniac from Leap 2. From the look on her face I could see she was in a daze, barely able to believe what was about to happen.

Let me set the table for you. Alone on one side of the eight-foot long setting was John around the corner to my left. On the far end of the rectangular table was Bob directly across from me. He faced all the sophisticated stuff that ultimately would capture and bring the precious words which followed to the public. To Bob's left around the corner was Christine. To her left getting closer to me was Eugene, then Don was next to my buddy and business partner, Robert Brooks.

As the theme music rolled in Bob's headphones, he proclaimed, "We're coming down in three...two...one."

"Welcome to the Leap of Sports Radio Show!" I quipped. I went into the normal schpeel about the program taking a look at faith, family and football with regard to the Green Bay Packers. Then I cut to the chase.

"The Gang." From left, Eugene Robinson, Don Beebe, Robert Brooks, Steve Rose and John Michels

"Boy, do we have some surprise guests with us. Eugene Robinson is here today."

"What's up? What's happening?" smiled the always jovial Packer safety.

"Also Don Beebe is here, Don say 'hey'."

"Hey, how ya doin," chimed the speedy receiver.

"And Robert Brooks is here. Brother, how are ya?"

"I still love ya, Steve," said Brooks with a tender smile and eyes twinkling as we shared the same microphone.

"Hey, our book is coming out this week, How 'bout that?"

"It's gonna be good, I can't wait. Where's my copy? I should get one before everybody," he giggled.

"It comes off the press on Wednesday and we're gonna have a real good time talking about your miracle." I was referring to his incredible recovery from a devastating knee injury the previous season.

Amidst all the hoopla I almost forgot to bring in my friend, my rock, and my savior (as far as this radio stuff goes).

"John, how are you my friend?"

"I'm doing great, Steve."

It was a rare day for more reasons than the obvious. One of the really different things was that this particular show was following a loss. The Pack had quite a string of victories which dated all the way back to the last loss which had occurred in Dallas in 1996. I addressed it right away.

"Guys, as I woke up today it was one of those days where I'm glad I don't put my faith in people," I said. I was referring to the fact that if we put our faith in anything else but God, ultimately we get let down. I let the forum open to whomever wanted to attack this first. It was John.

"Well, it's one of those circumstances where you look at the fans and people around you and a lot of people are depressed today because we lost a game yesterday. I'm just thankful that I don't play this game for man, that I play this game for God cause I'd be one of those people down in the dumps, too."

I reflected on the fact that God will cause all things to work together for good. He tells us this in Scripture in Romans 8:28, a verse that John signs along with his autograph. He agreed as I brought it up. We had one guy who knew how this all works. Don Beebe had played on four losing Super Bowl teams. I asked him to talk about it.

"Well after last season, (the Super Bowl win with the Packers) to tell

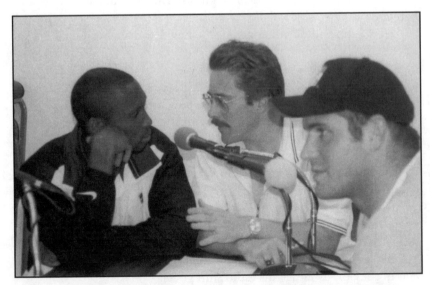

Steve enjoys a quiet moment with Robert in the Winners Success Radio Network Studio. John is at right.

you the truth, I forgot about it," he said laughing.

"Praise God for that," I said.

"I'm just kidding," joked Beebe. "When you lose the Super Bowl, which nobody on this team has experienced, you feel like your whole season was for naught. Going to four straight Super Bowls was a great accomplishment even though we didn't win it, but, on the other hand, to be a part of something like that was just awesome."

It was time to bring in the charisma of Eugene Robinson who was in his second year with the Packers since coming in a trade from Seattle. I asked him when it was that he noticed that this team was a little bit different from any others he's been a part of.

"I think my first training camp. Last year I just couldn't believe how spiritual the team was and I say that in a "quote unquote" sense because everybody talks about God, but this team, I mean people would talk in the locker room about Jesus. I thought, man, that's kinda different."

Then he said something that captured what has been my vision and understanding about how God is paying attention to Green Bay.

Robinson added, "And then when we started practicing, I said, 'Man, God must have his hand on this team', cause this team just clicks on all cylinders. A team that's real sensitive toward the Lord and one another. I thought that was real unique as an outsider looking in," he concluded.

I passed the same ball to Brooks as to just when he knew he was in Packermania land.

"I took probably a year. My first year I was just in awe of being in Green Bay. We didn't play very well, but the fans were still 100% no matter what. In the off season it was still crazy; that's when I realized there was something special here," said the South Carolinian.

Michels commented that he could tell from his vantage point from USC that this was a special bunch. After his first minicamp in 1996 he really got a dose of how special this was. Especially Reggie White's influence.

We shifted to talking about how important winning is. I commented how Reggie had straightened me out on this issue the year before - that winning truly is important. As Reggie once told me, "Steve, people don't wanna listen to losers." What did Don Beebe think?

"Well that's just the way society is. What Reggie said is true; that people want to listen to a winner and be associated with a winner. If you're a loser and you go 1-15, you know you're not gonna be listened to. The season that we had has opened up a lot of doors for me to go out and talk about my faith," elaborated Don.

Eugene finished the segment saying, "That's why I think people will remember a Super Bowl, but even though they don't remember we won at such and such a time, God's given us a platform where people will be led to Christ because we won a Super Bowl."

Bob indicated it was time for a break and rolled the bumper music. During the break, which is actually just a stop in the taping, Eugene chatted with Christine and wrote something on a napkin. Beebe and John chatted while Robert and I caught up on what had been happening.

After the break we took time to talk about something that doesn't come up much during the show---Packer football. Brooks pointed out that, although they'd lost to the Eagles the day before, God had his "hand on this team and the Packers would do well during the season."

Beebe noted that when you win the Super Bowl each team would be "gunning for you." He was right. Robinson chimed in that we win and lose as a team. Michels said a critical analysis of the game and being real about the performance would allow them to quickly bounce back. They did. But, was and is winning important for the Packers? Sort of.

One of the points I'd begun to make early in the season came out. It's become the signature phrase between John and me. It boils down to this question which I posed to the listeners and the guys. "In a hundred years from now is it gonna matter to any of us if we won a Super Bowl or not?" No. We all agree that all that would matter is if we were covered by the blood at Calvary.

What are the Packers of today doing to "sharpen their saws" and to let "iron sharpen iron" so they are not only out fighting the physical battle on the football field but the spiritual battle as well so as to present their message to a watching world? Eugene went first.

"Reggie White will call what we call 'Saturday Night Live' meetings where we get together (in White's room) and pray and have Bible time. It's standing room only so you better get there quickly or you won't get a seat. Just ask Don Beebe."

Beebe smiled and acknowledged that he had recently come "just a tad" late to the meeting and found himself having to strain just to pop his head in the doorway.

The veteran safety continued to point out that this isn't the norm on other NFL football teams.

"I used to lead all the chapel services in Seattle and it was like pulling teeth to get five or six guys.   Here we have a chapel service in Philadelphia and there were thirty people there. More than half our team is represented and I'm not even counting the people in mass!" beamed Robinson. "At this given moment you have Packer players on Saturday or Sunday taking time for the Lord and that is unusual," he emphasized. "Most of the type of football players you hear about are egotistical, your "I-Me" type of guy and we're here takin' time to say, 'God, what would you have us do?' That's different."

That says a lot. Keep in mind that this is a Super Bowl caliber team. Keep in mind that when you're a star with fame and money, it can be tough to stay close to the Lord or even pay attention to God at all. Not in Green Bay.

Beebe played with several guys in Buffalo who were Christians, like Frank Reich and Steve Tasker, but Beebe noted a difference in Packerland.

"There are a few more guys here who are real committed and more of them. In Buffalo guys knew who the Christians were and we talked in the locker room, but here it's like part of the team." His next line belongs in the heart of the greatest leap of faith statements ever published. Don revealed something he felt in his soul then.

"I really believe this, and it may sound funny, but by the end of the year, or even next year---every Green Bay Packer might be a born-again Christian."

He laughed with excitement as John Michels quipped, "At the rate we're goin' now."

Beebe continued on his roll. "It's only the second week and I think we've had about six guys accept Christ. Without naming names, that's not the issue, but six guys have accepted Christ and that's powerful. Now--that's unbelievable!"

"There's a party going on in heaven, I can tell you that much!" celebrated Robinson in divine timing.

"Yeah," quickly echoed Don. "Eugene's right. You can't get a seat. I showed up ten minutes late to SNL and I had to sit by the doorway off in a corner and chapel's the same way. So I think it's out in the open here more than any other place I've been, but we had other committed groups there too," he finished.

Without realizing it, I was about to bust the group up for a bit as I insinuated that Robert Brooks was in the "twilight of his career" whereas Don and Eugene were a little more in the "walking into the sunset" part. Without losing a beat, facetiously yet somewhat seriously, Eugene took exception.

"You're not calling us old? What's goin' on, man?"

Brooks was laughing.

"You were trying to get a sneaky one in there," jabbed the great looking number 41. I responded and defended myself without hesitation.

"Gene, put it this way. In "dog years" you're about 89."

"Now I'm 89 in dog years!"

"And I'm 85, so..." noted Beebe who'd done some quick addition or multiplication.

"You're 85, uh, I'm older," finished Robinson.

It was time to talk about what was undeniably the greatest medical recovery in National Football League history. I speak of Robert bouncing back from his injury. He was about to talk about it. In Leap 2 he got into great detail, but was about to add more revelations to the story.

"Robert Brooks has an incredible fire for the Lord right now because he has had an off-season and quite a life since October 14 of 1996. Robert, you know, the Reader's Digest version is not necessarily fair here, but give us a glimpse of where the Lord has taken you since then, man."

Robert laughed with great joy to begin to tell his tale. "I think I'm on a entirely different level from where I was before with the Lord. I thank Jesus for that. If you read Leap of Faith, you need to read Leap of Faith 2, because there's no way I could sit here and explain to you where I am and why I am where I am, because I've been through a lot," explained Robert.

"What I've been through has brought me that much closer to the Lord. It's amazing. I can't even explain it. And like I told you when I sat down with you when we did Leap of Faith 2 that it wasn't me speaking (as he told me the story that summer) and it was not me, and I prayed that I would allow his Holy Spirit to move and to speak for me...and that's what happened. And everything I said in that book was totally true."

I reiterated the awesomeness of what really had happened and it took me back to that hot summer day on July 7, 1997, when he first shared the story. I got Brooks to unload some things he's never talked about before.

"In a nutshell, you spoke of how God in a dream (two weeks into the

Eugene chats with Don during a break in the "LOFSRS."
Both had their Bibles lying in front of them.

1997 season) told you that you weren't gonna be finishing the season. He led you through that whole process and told you He was gonna heal you."

"Right, I actually saw about a year-and-a-half of my life. It was deep. A lot of people ask me, 'How did I handle being injured and not playing in the Super Bowl so easily.' It was because God had shown me everything that was going to happen after that."

It gets more stunning as Brooks pressed forward to share about the guidance he had received from above.

"I knew I was gonna be healed. I knew we were gonna win the Super Bowl. I knew that I was gonna make it back to training camp. These are things I told people the day after I was injured because I had the revelation week two of the season."

Like the leading from the Lord that Reggie White has proclaimed over the years, Brooks talked about how the Holy Spirit in an inaudible voice spoke to his heart.

"When I say revelation, I didn't see anything. It was just like somebody was talkin' to me in a dream and I couldn't see anything. So I didn't know if I was gonna injure my knee or if it was gonna be a shoulder or if it was gonna be a concussion or whatever. All I knew was I wasn't gonna finish the season. The Packers were gonna win the Super Bowl. My status as a ball player was not gonna change; I was gonna be healed; I was gonna have a great testimony and a lot of people were gonna be comforted based on the way God would comfort me."

Wow! Did you catch that? Did you read that account anywhere? Of course not. Not only had the popular receiver told me he'd only shared it with Eric (his friend) and me, but it was just too bizarre for the media to handle. He knew because of my willingness to take the leap of faith in proclaiming God's hand is on this team that I wouldn't think he was crazy.

I couldn't help but point out another bit of prophecy from Brooks which, by this time, had already come to fruition. That same summer Robert had told me he was going to score a touchdown in the game on Monday Night Football against the Bears. He did. Honestly, he saw himself leaping into the stands before the national audience. So did I, but God had other plans.

I recalled the moment in the third quarter when he scored. "I told Kim, I said, 'Everybody look out, there he goes!' (to leap in the stands). You and I saw you leaping in the stands and guess what? God saw Robert Brooks giving glory to Him. Is that not what happened?" I asked.

Brooks confirmed this. "Exactly. Terry Mickens asked me if I was gonna jump in the stands. And I said, 'You know, I know I'm gonna get in the end zone because God has set the stage.' My first game back, it's on Monday Night Football, and the stage is set for me to glorify God. When I scored the touchdown I said, 'I'm not jumping in the stands; I'm giving this to God. This is his first 10% '" (Readers, you will recall that after that touchdown, Brooks knelt in the endzone to give Jesus the glory.)

I then acknowledged that he had told me he would score in that game. I didn't put it in Leap 2 just to protect him in case it didn't happen. I should have known better. Robert quickly smiled and reminded me.

"What did I tell you when we were doing the book, Leap of Faith 2? It's for real?" He was right; what could I say?

It was time to explain another miracle. How had John Michels come into the league and got a Super Bowl ring in his first year?

"Explain this to the panel of three, John, and me too." Beebe giggled as he waited in anticipation with Eugene and Brooks. With a twinge of embarrassment and a little blush on his face, the former rookie literally had to face the three to give account.

"I mean it is an amazing journey. You know I'm sittin'..." John hesitated sensing he was about to put his foot in his mouth but went ahead anyway.

"I'm sittin' across from three guys...." Like me earlier, innocently he had walked into an ambush as he spoke of the "seasoned veterans" with whom he'd shared the joy and from whom he took the heat in more than one way.

As loud laughter and gibberish chatter broke all over the room knowing John would have to "back track," Eugene was at it again. "He's gonna call me old now." The big man and co-host handled it admirably, I thought.

"I'm sitting across from three very experienced players. These guys have been around as Don was sharing before and had been to four Super Bowls and never'd had the opportunity to win one."

Off mic I asked Beebe, "Don, is he rubbin' it in there a little bit?" Michels, refusing to acknowledge my heckling, plunged forward.

"Gene was in a situation in Seattle where he had never gotten to a Super Bowl."

"I couldn't get there, baby!" confirmed the vibrant one.

"And here I am as a rookie coming in and winning in the first try and you know...the funny thing is Keith Jackson..." Beebe interrupted and said, "Come on, John, let me pull that silver spoon." The second year tackle continued.

"Keith Jackson, who's a great man of faith, shared with me last year after we won the Super Bowl 'I'm not talking to you anymore...cause (Michels now laughed) we've all fought so hard for this and you as a rookie getting your ring in the first try is not right.'"

Before we went into the break I shared how important it was for all of us to use the platform we'd been given. I pointed out that they (we) may never have it again. Unfortunately, those words would prove all too true as the season ended in San Diego four months later.

Eugene had to peel out to do his TV show and Robert had to split, too. Christine took a couple great pictures which will go down in the books as some of the sweetest in Packer history. You know, one thing I've always noticed is that when you take a picture with more than one player, sometimes the guys will act like a bunch of seventh graders. This was no exception.

In one, there's Don Beebe smiling cause he was on his tippy toes trying to "out tall" his teammates. (See picture "The Gang") Others also have been included from this historic program. After the break, Don finished up. I have chosen to include the incredible dialogue Beebe shared the following half hour in a chapter of his own in the Packer Hall of Faith. It's too pure, perfect and personal to not credit him personally. I don't want to share it here. The message itself warrants being dealt with outside of "The Gang" in order to give it its proper due. It contains, in my opinion, both a great story and the best one-liner ever, each exclusive from the other.

Christine Winkelmen, a great gal who I profiled in Leap 2, took the mic at the end of the show. She shared some of the struggles in being a youth leader. John complimented her on being one of the real leaders and role models for the kids. It was a rap. Don left.

As Bob Gardinier tore down the equipment, we just looked at each other and laughed. We couldn't believe it. We turned off the lights and walked away. Christine was still stunned and I knew we had one of the greatest programs ever recorded in Packer history. It doesn't take too much of a leap of faith to think that you might agree with that conclusion also.

I couldn't resist when I got home. Although I'd just seen Bob, I picked up the phone and called him. He answered. Without saying anything else, I simply asked him one more time, "Did that really happen this afternoon?" He assured me it had. I hung up the phone and just shook my head in incredulous disbelief and amazement.

CHAPTER 4

Ken Ruettgers
Turning Another Page

Flashback. It was a crisp September morning when I spied a 6-6, 292-pound giant walking toward me. All my cool left me as this big person's downward gaze locked on to my upward stare. My knees began to rattle like chattering teeth. His chest protruded like a bumper on a car. His biceps and forearms were like Popeye's. I thought, "Look at this...a gorilla with a t-shirt and shorts on!" Then he stuck out his paw to grab mine.

"Hi, I'm Ken Ruettgers of the Green Bay Packers," he professed confidently. Being a man of total unflappability and a man of a million words---I forgot my name! I thought he would have to pick me up as one would an ice sculpture and then sit me in my chair. I must have found my seat by myself. Eventually, I snapped out of it and actually began a conversation with my new friend.

"Ken, I thou..thought we could talk about some of these things," I babbled as I looked at some of my notes for the first radio show we would ever do together. He sat down and proceeded to shatter every stereotype of a Green Bay Packer multimillionaire I had ever possessed. I confess that I was both scared and somewhat skeptical as to the type of man I was going to meet that day. In a matter of minutes he relieved me of every anxiety.

"Steve, I'm gonna stop at the Shell Station on my way here each week

*Ken Ruettgers
and Steve Rose
in Ken's office.*

before the show. I was wondering, what kind of coffee and doughnut you would like me to bring you?" At that moment I would have been safer had I been locked in a high chair because I just about fell off of my stool. His words were not what I expected at all.

Astounded at what I had just heard, I replied, "Ahhh...how about a white longjohn and some decaffeinated coffee?" I really thought he was kidding. I mean, if he would have asked me to lay out the carpet and be ready with anything for him, I would have done it. After all, he was a Green Bay Packer.   You know what? Each week my new friend would come in with goodies from the Shell Station or Hardees, just as he said he would.

It is significant that Ken did precisely what he said he would do. Since then, everything Ken Ruettgers has told me he would do he has done. Fact of the matter is, he wouldn't have had to cater to me at all. I would have happily followed him around like a little puppy dog caring for his and the other Packer guests' needs if they would have wanted me to.

What was the first thing Ken Ruettgers taught me about himself? He had come to serve, not to be served. I have never forgotten his first words of outreach with the "doughnut" question, nor will I ever, ever forget Ken Ruettgers. He is, in my opinion, one of the greatest reflections of Jesus Christ of all the Packers I have come to know in my ministry with them. Ken was the first to smash some of the "stereotypes" I had brought to the studio that morning back in '94. Many of the brothers on the team continued to do the same over the years.

As I recall what has transpired in both Ruettgers' and my life since then, I now realize that the day of our first meeting together was the beginning of my love affair with a select group of God-fearing men on the Packers. Why had God chosen Ken Ruettgers to be the man to introduce me to my fresh and new calling? Only God knows, but I'm delighted and blessed that He did.

In research for this book, as in Leap 1 and 2, I felt it was imperative that I get insight and feedback from my friend. With that thought in mind, I picked up the phone and played a game of Russian roulette. Is Ken in town or somewhere else around the country? According to Ken, he doesn't travel that much, but it seems to me that he's always somewhere when I try to contact him. But I was fortunate on this day.

"Hello," said the big man with an even deeper enthusiasm than I'd ever heard in the past.

"Ken, it's Steve. How you doing?"

"Great, what's goin' on?"

"Ken, I'm writing Leap 3 and want some ideas. I also want to talk to you about the Packer Hall of Faith. Ken, you're going in!"

"How long do you have to be out of the game before you're inducted?" he laughed.

"It's immediate," I revealed. "No waiting period for the Packers here who are a part of the 'God Squad.'" Ken agreed to serve with me on the induction committee. I also wanted to give Ruettgers' fans an update of how he was doing in his life since his retirement from football on November 20, 1998. The many calls and letters that I have received over the years from Leap 1 and 2 readers predominately center around Ken.

"Come on over to the house at 10 a.m. Wednesday."

"You're on," I said gleefully. Normally, I would have let him go, but I couldn't help but ask why there was an added spark in his spirit.

"Ken, you sound like a million bucks. How do you feel?"

"Aw, great, the Lord has given me a new direction. I'm taking a job in author relations with Multnomah Books!" This was the publisher of Ken's bestselling book, <u>Homefield Advantage: A Dad's Guide to the Power of Role Modeling</u>, released in August of 1995. It has sold 25,000 copies.

"Congratulations!," I beamed. "I'm proud of you. If there's anybody who deserves it, Kenny, it's you."

"Well, thanks, Steve," he finished. I let him go in anticipation of our meeting.

I made my way up Highway 41 from Neenah to Green Bay. It's a pretty drive anytime of the year, but during the summer, it's downright gorgeous. Forty minutes later I pulled up to the Ruettgers' abode on the west side of Green Bay. I had no sooner stepped out of the car when I heard a familiar voice.

"Hey, Steve!" It was Sheryl, Ken's bride of twelve years. She was visiting with a neighbor across the street.

"Where's the big man?" I asked carrying my briefcase across the lawn to the front door.

"He's in the house waiting for you," she told me. Sure enough, there

Steve shares a laugh with Ken and Sheryl Ruettgers in their Green Bay home.

he was standing in the doorway. Not only was Ken there to meet me, but so was his older daughter, Katherine, who is eight. I noticed she had a cast on her left arm.

"What did you do?" I asked.

"I fell down and broke it."

There was no sign of Susan, 6, the youngest of the Ruettgers three children. Matt, 10, was at a football camp.

We walked down the hallway and into Ken's office, the same one we had walked into after a couple of the old "Timeout" shows back in 1994. A much different, more secure, down-sized Ruettgers hobbled ahead of me. His left knee was wrapped in an ace bandage and the aluminum crutches which braced him glaringly declared that the game of football will follow him forever. He had just had his fifth knee surgery.

Ken once told me in 1996 that the pain in his cartilageless knee left him feeling as if he had the worst toothache from his waist to his foot. As I watched him, it occurred to me that this is what NFL players mean when they say they will take aches and pains to their graves.

Wearing a blue Super Bowl XXXI t-shirt and light green hat, blue jean shorts and his usual Reeboks, he told me to "grab a chair."

I slid down into the cushion of the seat which faced Ken. Gone from the room were the many game balls I'd remembered seeing there a few years ago. Gone was the picture of him and Brian Noble, which was taken for a Coca-Cola photo shoot in New York. I didn't inquire, but maybe their removal was part of moving on. Speaking of that, we talked about what he had told me just days earlier.

"We're moving in about a month," he proclaimed.

I guess I wasn't surprised. After all, I knew Multnomah was near Portland, Oregon. He told me he was going to be helping authors in their quest to promote their projects. He knows what that's like. He's been there.

We chatted about some of the people we would be including in the Packer Hall of Faith. He gave me some ideas and agreed to have a few of the guys from whom I needed to receive material call me. As we looked out the window we noticed a storm had rolled in. Within minutes, it was pouring. The lights flickered off and on once just as a pretty lady peeked into the room through the sliding doors.

"You look like a drowned rat, girl," I teased Sheryl while walking toward her. She clearly hadn't beaten the raindrops across the street.

"You don't want to touch me, I'm soaked," she said. I didn't care. I hugged her anyway. Sheryl Ruettgers, a sweet, petite brunette, is a Godly woman who is probably just as responsible for Ken's success as he is. Their love for each other was quickly apparent to me as I observed them the first day I met her. The affection they feel for and devotion they display toward one another should be the norm for every marriage.

As Ken and I continued our visit, I noticed his bookshelf held both a hard and soft copy of <u>Leap of Faith: God Must Be A Packer Fan.</u> (Personally, I think it's sign of intelligence when people have my books in their library.) I made a mental note that I needed to bring him a copy of <u>Leap of Faith 2: God Loves Packer Fans</u>. Ken leaned back and swiveled lightly to his left and peered out the window which was being washed by the storm.

"We're really going to miss Green Bay." He pointed to adjacent houses and talked about the special people in each one, what they do, and how they would be missed. The fact that Sheryl and Ken had stayed in Wisconsin as long as they had was somewhat of a mystery anyway. Both Ken's and Sheryl's families are in California and the families were commuting regularly. The only surprise was that they weren't going back to California, but to Oregon.

One thing I know with certainty about Ken Ruettgers. He will only take his family where God wants them to go. I could tell that Ken was feeling good about where he was and was relieved that God had given him a new direction with his career.

"Being financially secure at 35 has given us some options, but we want to be sure to do what God wants us to do and to go where God wants us to go," he shared. I know Ken and his family are moving out of obedience to the Lord. They will be missed greatly by this community.

After an hour of great counsel, a few laughs and suggestions for this book Ken's phone rang. Sheryl said it was Ken's mentoree, John Michels.

"What's up, bud?" he asked.

"Yeah, I'll pick you up in ten minutes. Steve and I are just finishing up and he will follow us over there." Michels had agreed to speak to a group of football campers at Green Bay Community Church.

We continued our philosophical discussion about God all the way out to Ken's Suburban. He finished a thought as he leaned on his crutches and the door of his truck. I had promised myself I would remember what the discussion was about so I could share it with you. I can't. Trust me,

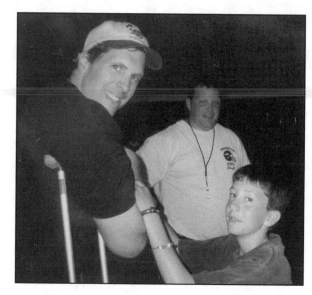

Matthew Ruettgers (10) with his proud dad. Check-out Matt's WWJD bracelet.

though, it was good. Except for the radio transcriptions, I have written this and the previous two books from photographic memory. I guess I ran out of film in that moment!

As I followed behind Ken to the football camp, I was impressed by the fact that Ken's "white Suburban of salvation" (which I called it in an earlier book) was the same vehicle we had peeled around in to restaurants or to our favorite hangout, the Dairy Queen, back in 1994. If there is a guy who could be "freshening up" his wheels every year, it certainly could be Ken. It's not about that for him. It's about being a good steward of what God has given the Ruettgers.

Within minutes we were at John Michels' home. He waved to me as he hopped in with Ken. We got there a bit early, so the three of us sat in Ken's truck and visited. There we were, the two from USC and me. I could never imagine being in better company. Here were two giants in the eyes of the community, each with a common goal to serve Jesus Christ and honor Him in everything they do.

It suddenly dawned on me that I may never again have the opportunity to be with both Ken and John in the same place at the same time. I felt compelled to share what was on my heart.

"Hey, thanks Ken and John for what you guys have done for my ministry." These were the two men who gave me the chance to penetrate the inside of the team in order to share what God is doing. They were much too humble and modest to respond, but I think they knew what I was trying to say.

John did a great job with the kids at the football camp and among the campers was Ken's boy, Matthew. He wants to be the next Robert Brooks. Wearing a WWJD bracelet above his black catching gloves which wide receivers wear, he leaned on his dad proudly. We snapped a picture of the two. Then we left. I walked Ken and John to the lot and we split.

In early July I faxed Ken to tell him that I was going to be having knee surgery similar to the five he has had. I was scheduled for surgery at Mercy Medical Center in Oshkosh for the afternoon of July 9. The evening prior, I was pounding words into the computer for this book when, at about 10:15 p.m., the phone rang.

"Hello," I answered after hobbling up the steps.

"Steve, Ken Ruettgers. You're having surgery tomorrow, huh?" he responded so gently. Just back in town, here was the greatest role model I'd ever experienced in the history of my ministry on the phone comforting me because he's been there.

"The first time it's a little scary, but you'll be okay." he comforted. I listened to him, not so much for what he was telling me about the procedure, but because I was so moved by the softness of this former football beast's heart. I wanted to talk about the possibility of breakfast the following week.

"Right now, let's get you through tomorrow. It's gonna be a big day," he said softly. "I'll say a prayer for you." I know I was being shown a special side of Ken Ruettgers which few others have had the joy and privilege to experience.

Here is what the Packer books and some of the fans may remember about Ken Ruettgers. He was good... never a Pro-Bowler, but consistently one of the best offensive tackles in the NFL from 1985-1996. Only five other Packers have spent more time in a green and gold uniform. He's a shoo-in to the Packer Hall of Fame. By virtue of the fact that Ken is in the Packer Hall of Faith, I will recall something about Ken which is much more significant. He had one question he used to ask people.

"If you were to die today and stand before God and He would ask you 'Why should I let you into my heaven,' what would your answer be?'" What a great question! It's really the only one that matters.

Ken and his family will make a quiet exit from their Green Bay neighborhood and those who have come to love them. What have I learned from Ken? First and foremost, it is that a personal relationship with Jesus Christ is the most exhilarating experience in the world. Outside of that, life is a purposeless and meaningless series of practical jokes. I want what Ken Ruettgers has, his spirit, his heart and his compassion. Ken has shown me that it is great to be exactly who I am, and not be envious of who he, or any other person, is. In our early days together, Ken took a leap of faith to trust me. The Kingdom of God will never be the same.

In completion of this tribute to him, I can say that I will miss Ken Ruettgers. I won't be alone. I'd really like to be at Austin Straubel Airport in Green Bay to say goodbye and thank Ken one more time for all that he has done. I can tell you this - that as that plane heads west, a part of my heart will be on it. My comfort and gift from the Lord is that a big piece of Ken Ruettgers will have been left with me.

I have only a few words for my former partner, current role model and brother in Christ. "Ken, thank you. If I never see you again this side of heaven, I can say, 'Lord, thank you for the time we had together.' I also forgive you for introducing me to Ben & Jerry's ice cream, thus causing me to stumble "by the quart" from time to time. So few of us have had the opportunity to spend quality time around genuine goodness, but I can say that I have with you. And for that I am ever so grateful. So long, my friend. I will never forget you."

Can I ask you a question?" is what Ken Ruettgers asks
those who want an autograph. Those who have read the
"Leap" books know how important that question is.

CHAPTER 5

The Packer Hall of Faith

It's not about football. It never has been and never will be for a select group of men who have labored in the trenches of Lambeau Field. These men will be inducted into the Packer Hall of Faith, not to be confused with the Packer Hall of Fame. Many have striven for the success and recognition of induction into the Hall of Fame; but there are those who see the honor of induction into God's Hall of Faith. You may never have heard of it, but it has existed eternally.

Of those who have been inducted into the Packer Hall of Fame, any one of them will tell you that the Packer Hall of Faith is a greater honor. One of the inductees shared, "To be inducted into the Packer Hall of Fame is indeed a tremendous honor. But to be inducted into God's Hall of Faith is the most important thing that has happened in my life."

Current, as well as past, Packer notables will be the ones acknowledged in the next pages. Of special interest is the fact that there has been room designated for coaches, trainers and even fans, which is something new! (To the best of our knowledge the Packer Hall of Fame doesn't include fans)

The Packer Hall of Faith is merely a room, a division if you will, of God's Hall of Faith. He created it for all of His people, Packer fans or others, but only those who make the right choice can be inducted. That includes you, whether you are a Packer fan or not.

However, for many of the Packer fans reading this, we do have a special place for you in the Packer Hall of Faith. Stay with us for the details.

When we think of the Green Bay Packer Hall of Fame we think of the Starrs, Nitschkes and Kramers. The Whites and Favres and Ruettgers will be there someday, too. The criteria for entrance there is based on performance as a player. The Packer Hall of Faith is much different. The qualifications are much simpler. As we said, it's a choice... a leap of faith.

The benefits for the players, coaches, trainers and fans alike will be discussed in detail in the last chapter written by Pastor Arni Jacobson. Here are the qualifications for entrance into the Packer Hall of Faith for all listed here in this book and for those who would like to be included.

1. *An acceptance of Jesus Christ as Savior*
2. *A commitment to Jesus Christ as Lord*
3. *A personal relationship with Jesus Christ*

All individuals featured, like those of the Hall of Fame, have brought talent to Green Bay, but more importantly, they brought with them a sincere heart for God. Many of these saints of God had life-changing experiences once they accepted God's promise to make them sinless before Him. It happened through a conscious act of faith in their hearts to accept the saving blood of Jesus Christ which was shed at Calvary.

These are men with a mission and an agenda. From Carroll Dale and Bart Starr to John Michels and Robert Brooks, their lives have not really been about catching, running, or throwing a football. That's been their platform, but more aptly put, these Christians have been called to the ministry of sharing what God has done for them. They are God's chosen role models and leaders in the world of professional sports.

These are men who have put "feet to their faith." They live it first, preach it second; no one can accuse them of hypocrisy. Eugene Robinson's philosophy says it best, "What you do speaks so loud no use hearing what you have to say!" It's about doing it rather than saying it.

The men about whom you will read throughout this section are not perfect. I like what Sean Jones said in 1994 to me. "I'm not perfect, just forgiven. We, as born again believers, are just sinners in recovery."

That's says it all. Don't ask any of these people to judge another player. They have found that the occupation itself is full of enough struggles and temptations so that each has learned not to look at the speck in another's eye without seeing the log in his own.

In some cases presented, you will note their careers were far from smooth. Quite the contrary, several have had their faith tested through temptation or adversity. Before you read further, do yourself (and the players) two favors. First, take the players off the pedestal if you haven't already done so. They don't want to be there. It's too far down and too easy to fall. Second, raise yourself up a notch by realizing that God's purpose for your life is just as important as Reggie White's or Robert Brook's.

Let me clarify something at this point. There are many more people, I'm sure, who belong in this book, but I do not know who they are. Those you will read about here are only the ones I know of. Many you will recognize are players and friends that have crossed paths with me and my ministry. If you know of someone else who belongs, let me know. We'll be sure to include them, okay?

You will note I've included some information about each of them. You'll see everything from the name of the college they attended to their height and weight as a Packer. Some of it may help you to recall them, but much of it is just to let you know more about them and their unique ministries. One thing you won't see here is statistics. Why? Who cares? Will stats matter a hundred years from now to you or to them? Of course not, but what we hope is that everything used to fill space in this book will matter in eternity.

You may ask, "What's in this chapter for me?" Here is the good, no, great news. Along with these players you can be inducted also! That's right. This Hall of Faith has plenty of room for you, too. The induction ceremony is out of this world, the gifts that come with it are incredible, including a guarantee that someday you will meet Reggie White. Pretty cool, huh? Read on because further details are coming. Your induction papers are being prepared! They are only a few pages, a choice and a leap of faith away.

The Packer Hall of Faith
• THE LAMBEAU WING •

John Anderson

Born: February 14, 1956
Died:

Green Bay Packers   1978-1989
 #59   Linebacker
Michigan
Drafted GB first round 1978
HT: 6-3   WT: 228

Academic All-American at Michigan. Environmental education major. Named NFL "Man of the Year" by fans in 1983 for his efforts on behalf of civic and charitable causes. Loves fishing...fishing and fishing.

Inducted into the Packer Hall of Fame as a player 1996

Inducted into the Packer Hall of Faith as a player 1998

Known as a consummate and committed professional during his days with the Green Bay Packers, John Anderson continues to be a man whose character is above reproach. The same intensity with which he dedicated himself to his profession can be seen as John pours himself into sharing his faith.

A magazine interview done at the completion of John's career reported John to be a deeply religious person who often discusses his beliefs during speaking engagements. The tone of the article gave one the feeling that John was as crazy as someone who reported seeing little green men. John is not about "religion." What he is about is"relationship" with Jesus Christ. There is a difference.

It was December 10, 1996, when I had the privilege of speaking at a Fellowship of Christian Athletes banquet in Milwaukee. Waiting for me, in fact holding the door as a servant to let me in, was John Anderson. I had met him a few months earlier at WITI TV 6 in Milwaukee where he was employed. It was obvious why Ken Ruettgers had so many great things to say about John Anderson. Ken and John had roomed together during the end of John's and the beginning of Ken's careers.

Here's what the world of Packer fans may remember about Anderson. He was born in the great state of Wisconsin in Waukesha. After a tremendous prep career at Waukesha South he dared to go to Michigan to play for the rather volatile but undeniably great Bo Schembechler.

John was drafted in 1978 in the first round by the Packers. He contributed until the twelfth game of his baptismal season when he broke his arm. This was only the beginning for his faith to be tested. The following year, in July, he broke it once more...and then again in November of 1980! After remedial surgery in late 1980 (a bone was taken from his hip and grafted in his arm) his career continued with less frustration. However, he did break a leg in 1986.

One of the most disciplined players in Packer history, Anderson made quite a name for himself. Trust me when I tell you he had some tremendously impressive statistics. His "numbers," however, won't mean a thing someday, and he'd be the first to say so.

Here's what God has recorded. Not only did John take the greatest leap of faith by accepting Christ's sacrifice at the cross, but then he used his platform as a player to honor Him. Ken Ruettgers recalls how much of an impact John Anderson had on his life.

"John had a great, positive influence on my life. He really helped to mature me in Christ."

Ken Ruettgers wrote in his 1995 book, <u>Homefield Advantage,</u> that Anderson would choose one person from the locker room each year and pray for him. Ken Ruettgers happened to be one of them and Ruettgers is glad that he did.

Following Anderson's football career, many saw him as a TV analyst on the statewide broadcasts of Packer football. He also worked with WITI TV 6 in Milwaukee. Today, no longer in TV, he is pursuing other opportunities.

I know I said I wouldn't discuss statistics, but one is really "cool." In 1979 the Packers lost their kicker. Guess who filled in? As an ex-Punt, Pass and Kick champion he was ready. In his only attempt, he nailed a 39-yard kick! The fans were thrilled, but not nearly as much as were the angels on the day Anderson hurled his heart through God's golden goal posts. It was on that day that God nailed John's name on the wall in the Hall of Faith, the only award that matters to John Anderson.

The Packer Hall of Faith
• THE LAMBEAU WING •

Don Beebe

Born: December 18, 1964
Died:

Green Bay Packers   1996-1997
#82   Wide Receiver
Chadron State
Drafted third round, Buffalo 1989
HT: 5-11   WT: 185

Has given to the Make A Wish Foundation. Honored as "Unsung Hero" at NFL Banquet in 1997. Hobbies include golf and fishing.

Inducted into the Green Bay Packer Hall of Faith as a player 1998

Like many of the stories you will read about in the Packer Hall of Faith, this one defies most of the odds. He was considered small; he came out of Chadron State; but Don Beebe's story is worth sharing. No, it's not the football story you'll want to hear, but what God has chosen to do through this man because of his faithfulness that's worth noting.

I first had the privilege of meeting Don Beebe during the 1996 season. He and John Michels handled the co-hosting duties for the radio show as Ken struggled with his decision whether to play or to retire. I recall hitting it off well with the man they have called "White Lightning." Quite simply, he's white and he's fast...really fast. Don shared some things after a show.

"Steve, you've got to hear my story," he said to me. "You won't believe it." Once I heard it, I didn't. There were college eligibility disasters. He and wife Diana went to Chadron with virtually no money. It is a remarkable story of how God chose to use a man because he made himself available to Him. Don told us how an on-the-sport NFL tryout changed his life. At it, he ran a 40-yard dash in record time---barefoot!

We build the case here that God honored Don Beebe's commitment which came early in his life when he accepted Christ and chose to serve Him. With a strong Christian upbringing, he developed the courage and discipline to endure. He was rewarded with a great career that included being a part of five Super Bowl teams. He won a Super Bowl ring with the Packers, his first ever, in Super Bowl XXXI. But rings are not important to Don. Sharing his faith, however, is.

The premise of Don Beebe's life may have been ordained by God and exemplified by Beebe's response to one play. Many of you will recall the Super Bowl XXVII play in which Beebe's never-say-die actions actually changed many lives. The Pack was trailing by 35 points against the Cowboys when Beebe chased down Leon Lett after a fumble recovery from 25 yards behind him. Beebe swatted the ball out of his hands and through the end zone. Minor? Not at all.

"I got so much mail after the game from dads telling me that the play demonstrated to their kids to never give up. I tell people you never know when your one play may come," said the speedy one.

Because of Don's hard work, dedication, and credibility, he has had many opportunities to share his testimony and other stories. People listen. They should. Don shared two of the most profound things ever expressed in the history of the "Leap of Faith Sports Radio Show."

During week three, 1997, flanked by pals Eugene Robinson and Robert

Brooks, he gave people the real scoop. "I share with people that, you know, I'm not going to be able to take my material things, including my Super Bowl ring, to heaven, but I can take you!" It was breathtaking. Within minutes all in the studio and in the audience were riveted with intrigue and fascination as Beebe shared this story.

"My friend, Jeff, whom I have known since I was a kid, made a confession to accept Christ last October. Well, in February he was killed by a drunk driver. As his wife stood by his casket with the pastor she remarked, 'I want to know that I'll see him again.' The pastor said, 'You can.' She said, 'How?' He said, 'By trusting Christ as your Savior.'"

In one of the greatest stories ever told on radio, Beebe continued with the story of this God-appointed miracle. "So, she prayed to receive Jesus Christ right there over his dead body," he said softly. "Now, many people would have thought that it was his death that was a tragedy, but if he hadn't died, she may have been headed to hell and he would have already been in heaven. Now, my friends, that would have been a tragedy!" Amen.

Don Beebe's reign as a Packer ended after the 1997 season. God gave him other work to do. But we praise the Lord for giving us Packer fans Don for two years. Don Beebe, welcome. Take your place forever in the Packer Hall of Faith.

The Packer Hall of Faith
• THE LAMBEAU WING •

Robert Brooks

Born: June 23, 1970
Died:

Green Bay Packers   1992 -
#87   Wide Receiver
South Carolina
Drafted GB third round 1992
HT: 6-0   WT: 180

Earned B.S. degree in retailing. Has his own record label called, Shoo-in 4 Life Records, Inc., located in Columbia, S.C. Released a song called, "Jump" in 1996. Regularly does Robert Brooks Football Camps. Spokesperson for Salvation Army, Red Cross and the Leukemia Society. Enjoys charity work "pertaining to God." Unofficial team barber.

Inducted into the Green Bay Packer Hall of Faith as a player 1998

Those who know Robert Brooks as a football player will describe him as resilient, remarkable and disciplined. For those of us who have been fortunate to have gotten to know the man, he is simply lovable. Born in Greenwood, South Carolina, this humble young man certainly has his priorities in order these days. It wasn't always that way.

Since entering the NFL Robert Brooks has had his share of struggles and, as he admits, one of the biggest struggles was with what he called his "bedroom faith."

"I would be in my room praying and reading the Bible, but I wouldn't go out and share my faith with others," he once confessed. That changed dramatically on October 14, 1996.

With apologies to those who have already read "Rise and Jump Again" from Leap 2, and are therefore familiar with the story, Brooks' whole life changed in a moment. You may want to refer to it, but here is the Readers Digest version.

On Monday Night Football he suffered what should have been a career- ending injury. It was not after total reconstructive surgery that he made one of the most amazing recoveries in NFL history, according to trainer Pepper Burruss. To say it was a medical marvel would not be stretching it at all. It was a miracle, pure and simple.

"We've seen anterior cruciates come back before and we have seen the patellar tendon come back before," said the veteran trainer, "but never the two together. It is the most remarkable recovery I have ever seen in my 20 years as a trainer."

While everyone was surprised, Brooks was not. His faith, now amplified because of Christ's healing touch on his knee, made him an absolutely new person. Today, all he wants to do is talk about God and how He sent His Son Jesus Christ to die for all of us. What he most wants to do is give God the glory.

It is with great pleasure that the man who perfected the "Lambeau Leap" and graced the covers of Leap 1 and 2, takes one more leap right into the front row of the Packer Hall of Faith.

The Packer Hall of Faith
• THE LAMBEAU WING •

Pepper Burruss

Born: April 15, 1954
Died:

Green Bay Packers since 1992-
Began 1977 with NY Jets
Head Trainer
Purdue, Northwestern University

Served two terms on the executive committee of the
Professional Football Athletic Trainers Society (PFATS)
One term as AFC assistant trainer rep and one year as
NFC head trainer rep.

Inducted into the Packer Hall of Faith as a trainer 1998

From the moment we met, I admired him. Pepper Burruss is the head trainer of the greatest group of football players in the world. What's more exciting is that he is a Christian amidst the largest congregation of born-again believers disguised as a football team.

I have gone on record on radio, TV and in my books to say that it is absolutely no coincidence that it was Pepper Burruss who helped peel the paralyzed Dennis Byrd off the Jet carpet; that he "called" Reggie's elbow miracle in 1994; and that he was there when Robert Brooks' destroyed knee was healed.

He was born in Beacon, New York. I have no idea how the name "Pepper" started, although I have noticed that his hair over the last five years does have a little more salt each year than in the previous one. Born Thomas "Pepper" Burruss, he is self-proclaimed "Thomas the doubter."

"I really need to see, feel and conceptualize things." Pepper has been a regular on the "Leap of Faith Sports Radio Show" each year since its inception. Kind, articulate and modest are terms that best describe this man. His well-timed sense of humor is both contagious and highly enjoyable.

As I sat with Pepper at his Packer office, he was quick to share how he feels "blessed" to have the job he has. He came to the Packers from the Jets in 1992. Neither job was gained by application, but by invitation. At Ron Wolf's insistence, he followed the Packer G.M. here from the "Big Apple."

He has nothing but great things to say about both Wolf and Coach Mike Holmgren. Of the greatest coach since Lombardi he comments, "The captain of this ship has the right center of the universe in Jesus Christ."

Burruss enjoys talking about when he accepted Christ as his Lord and Savior in April of 1977. He is not afraid to share his faith and is a gifted public speaker. In his talks to children he stresses the realities of peer pressure and how this can be positive.

The trainer tells youth that, "Peer pressure is a form of accountability. There is nothing wrong with peer pressure if it is good peer pressure. So it's important to carefully choose who your peers are."

For seven months there are virtually no off days for Pepper, but he has no complaints. When the football medicine cabinet is closed for Pepper, he looks forward to doing some catching up. "I look forward someday to taking a vacation in the fall. I want to make up for lost time and pick some apples."

Thomas "Pepper" Burruss has been a "salt" while in Green Bay. Always visible when he is flashed on national TV because of injuries on the field, he has been somewhat invisible, but no less impacting, when off the field.

"Pep", your corner has been prepared. When you're done, lay down the tape and the scissors and rest forever in the Packer Hall of Faith.

The Packer Hall of Faith
• THE LAMBEAU WING •

Carroll Dale

Born: April 24, 1938
Died:

Green Bay Packers   1965-1972
#84   Wide Receiver
Virginia Tech
Traded to Packers 1965
HT: 6-2   WT: 200

Endorsed "Super Touch" hand lotion while an NFL player. An avid outdoorsman and hunter. Education major in college. Today he is an Athletic Director in Wise, VA.

Inducted into the Packer Hall of Fame as a player 1979

Inducted into the Packer Hall of Faith as a player 1998

Carroll Dale was a good wide receiver while with the Packers. I vividly recall, while in fifth grade in 1970, Dale making a touchdown catch from a Don Horn bomb to beat the Atlanta Falcons. As great a receiver as he was, it looks like he was a better sender--of the gospel of Jesus Christ.

This became no more apparent than when he was invited to eulogize Ray Nitschke at his funeral on March 14, 1998. He spoke as Ray's friend, and as the one who had been the Packer linebacker great's roommate for the last eight years of Ray's career in Green Bay.

The Green Bay Packer stats will show that Dale scored 34 precious touchdowns, that he averaged 20 yards per catch while in a green and gold uniform. That's great, but not as great as his purpose for coming to Green Bay.

You see, one of the greatest Packer stories ever was planted in the heart of one Raymond Nitschke beginning in 1965. Dale and Ray spent time on the road together as Packers, a lot of time. Carroll would boldly share the gospel of Jesus Christ with Nitschke. Sometimes it takes a while for a seed to grow. Well, in 1995, Carroll's seed of truth took root, and Ray Nitschke accepted the Lord Jesus as his personal Savior.

It's never what it appears to be. God apparently sent Carroll Dale to Green Bay so that a receiver could help a linebacker receive the greatest gift ever. Mr. Dale, please accept this induction into the Green Bay Hall of Faith. Well done, thou good and faithful servant.

The Packer Hall of Faith
• THE LAMBEAU WING •

Ken Ellis

Born: September 27, 1947
Died:

Green Bay Packers   1970-1975
#48   Cornerback
Southern University
Packers 4th rd Draft in 1970
HT: 5-10   WT: 190

Worked in community relations with youth in association with the Baton Rouge police department. Has spoken to over 2 million young people. Received a Masters Degree in Education.

Inducted into the Packer Hall of Fame as a player 1998

Inducted into the Packer Hall of Faith as a player 1998

Ken Ellis is the first and only player to go into the Packer Hall of Fame and the Packer Hall of Faith in the same year! Remembered for his blinding speed, he came into the Packer organization as a wide receiver. After spending a few weeks behind Carroll Dale he switched sides of the ball and the rest, as they say, is history.

It was on opening day. The Packers were being slashed by the Detroit Lions when it happened. Detroit quarterback Greg Landry had a 78-yard quarterback sneak! I can remember the speedy cornerback collaring him after he ran him down from many yards from the other side of the Lambeau turf.

Things that matter to Packer fans might be that he earned All-Pro honors in 1972, '73 and '74 and was elected to the Pro Bowl in those same years. More importantly, he is a member of God's elect.

Birthed into both the Packer Hall of Fame and the Hall of Faith in 1998, he has no quams about acknowledging which is the greater. "It's a privilege to be inducted into the Green Bay Hall of Fame," said Ellis. "Like Paul Hornung, Ray Nitschke and others who have been inducted into the Pro Football Hall of Fame, it is a great honor. But to be inducted into God's Hall of Faith is the most important thing that has ever happened in my life."

Former Packer Mike McCoy presented Ellis in the Packer Hall of Fame. McCoy shared with me how Ellis touched him and his teammates. "He was a great, great teammate because he always encouraged everybody in the huddle and he was always there for you."

Today, Kenny is a minister at Bethany Prayer and Worship Center in Bethany, Louisiana, north of Baton Rouge. He is quick to point out that sports have helped him to adjust to his calling. "I think having played sports really helped me in the area of self-discipline," he observed. "The discipline you have to have as a minister in order to study the Scriptures and to seek God's counsel about different things is the same."

Ken, it is with great pleasure that the committee of the Packer Hall of Faith welcomes you with honors. Thanks for your faithfullness.

CHAPTER 6

Taking Stock in the Packers

You have to admit that it even outdid the time they sold dirt and grass. The Packers had done it again. This time they peddled next-to-worthless pieces of paper for $200 each! Remember after the 1996 championship against the Carolina Panthers, when the Packers sold turf from Lambeau field for $10 a box? It was marketed as "frozen tundra." People waited in line in deathly freezing temperatures to have the opportunity to make a purchase.

On November 13, 1997, the team took it a step further when they received the blessing from the 1,900 Packer stockholders to sell shares in the team. Reserve capital would be used to improve the facilities and not for salaries. Some would be saved for building a new stadium in the future. (Doesn't it seem inconceivable to think of the Pack playing in Green Bay anywhere else but at Lambeau Field?)

This venture would be the fourth stock sale in the history of this blessed franchise which has been plopped in the heart of what others may consider average America. Not the Lord.

The Packers informed the NFL in October of their intentions to raise capitol through the sale. Officials told Packer brass that as long as they stayed within a special set of parameters, they were grandfathered and did not have to undergo a league vote on the issue. This is something which is virtually impossible for any other team in the league to pull off. You can't even say, "Only in America." No, "Only in Green Bay!" You know, God just might be showing favor here after all!

Packer president Bob Harlan said, "One owner told me, 'I could never do that.' I told him he probably couldn't, but we're unique." How true! A person only has to inhabit these parts during a season to realize and to experience how the Packers meld into the fabric of the Green Bay community and the state, as well. You can read all you want about it, but it's something to see.

After getting the green light for the sale, Packer marketing people determined that it was quite likely the Packers should be able to sell up to one million shares of common stock in the team. However, the Packers appeared to have wanted to be conservative and set a goal considered to be a bit on the low end. They hoped to sell only 400,000 shares.

Price per share would be a mere $200. But here was the catch. There would be no dividends. That's right. There would be absolutely no chance to receive any return on the investment. Can a person sell it to get their money back? I'm not sure. For just $200 a Packermaniac could display on his wall an acknowledgment that he was in business with one of the great organizations on the planet.

Let's talk about this. There are a few mysterious, if not curious, questions. Who buys an investment like this with no value or dividend, and where? The answer is, of course, only a Packer backer, and only in Green Bay. Why? God only knows, but a hunch says it might be because this is a warm and fuzzy organization to which God is trying to draw attention. Such has been the case recently.

Let's run some numbers on this. Four-hundred-thousand shares at $200 a share. My seventh-grade Campbellsport Southwest education tells me that's $80 million dollars. Who else do you know can sell $80 million dollars' worth of anything while having to promise virtually nothing in return? You guessed it again. The consultants said it could be done, especially in Green Bay.

Those in business who are all too familiar with consultants will tell you that these people can make a few mistakes from time to time. Afterall, a consultant is usually a person who can't find a real job so... Okay, I'll give them the benefit of the doubt in this case. But, the numbers fell short of the estimates...way short.

From November of '97 till March of '98, the Packers received only an average of $200,000 per day or about $1.4 million per week for the 17 weeks of the campaign. What a shame to be so far below the projections. Even though the team averaged $700,000 per day or $4.9 million per week, the best they could do was $726,000 per day as fans purchased stock for the holidays.

By the week surrounding the Super Bowl in January, the sales dipped to only $117,000 per week. Surely with even Packer fans a loss in the Super Bowl should have affected the plans, right? Not according to Harlan.

"I think it had very little effect on it quite honestly. I thought the consistency of it was one of the things that made it most pleasant." He explained why. "It didn't drop after the loss to Indianapolis and it didn't go through the roof after the victory over Dallas." Consistency is the key here. Is it that Packer fans consistently are insane?

On March 17 of '98, Harlan addressed the media to announce that the team had 105,989 new partners encompassing all 50 states, which included from Guam to the Virgin Islands. I don't want to blow the whistle on anybody here, but 105,989 shares at 200 bucks a share is roughly a little more than $20 million. For virtually worthless paper, however, that's not bad, eh?

Now you may say, "Steve, you sound a bit facetious here." You would be right. Furthermore, you could say, "You sound a bit envious." And I'd say, "You got me, okay. If I was raising this type of dough for my ministry, well then, that would be different!" You're right. Really, think about it . . . $24 million going to a football team. Do you think all the families who purchased shares were in a position of financial security to do this? Maybe. All of them? I doubt it.

Friend, I love the Green Bay Packers. You know I do, but do these numbers we've just discussed tell a story of imbalanced priorities? I have to say that I believe they do. Don't shoot me, but I'd go so far as to suggest that a Packer share hanging on a person's wall just might be an indication that that person (assuming he/she made the purchase) has $200 too much!

Let me get my brother, Gary, in trouble so I don't have to take this wrap all alone. He's in the business of selling Packer-autograph memorabilia. Gary walked into my office last spring and tossed a Packer stock certificate frame on my chair.

"Here, if you know of anybody who has stock, sell them one of these. Tell them if they are "dumb enough" to buy worthless stock for $200, they can certainly afford $50 for a frame to display it." Would you agree there's some frightening truth in that sentence? Unfortunately so.

I'll be honest with you. I had everything I could do to battle the temptation to buy a share myself. Really! So, maybe I'm a little jealous, but I don't think so. I suppose if God is first in someone's life, what's a share of stock, huh? Maybe what bothers me is this "priority stuff." Unfortunately, I have a terrible gut feeling that too many people may have the certificate hanging in their office where the 10 commandments could be displayed. Or maybe it was thrown on top of a Bible which has been collecting dust?

Priorities. We all have them. What is impressive is that a group of Christians you're going to read about know that, like stock certificates, their Super Bowl rings will burn someday, too. All that matters is what has been invested into the Kingdom of Heaven. To a few of these special teddy bears who can be seen in Lambeau, that's all that really does matter.

When asked if the Packers were going to have another stock sale soon, Harlan insinuated it could be in another 25 years. Thank God, because I fear that I'll have just as much trouble resisting the urge to buy worthless paper then as I did during this last one.

CHAPTER 7

Big John

Some things just don't work out the way a person thought they would. Ask John Michels. His original dream did not come to fruiton. Today, however, he has accepted God's plan for his life. As a young man, Michels never envisioned himself in a professional football uniform, but a different one entirely.

Michels confessed, "You know, as a kid I wanted to be a gas station attendant. You had a uniform with your name on it. It seemed like he had a lot of friends and I just thought it would be a cool job."

Well shucks, these days the former USC grad dons much different duds at work. It's only a part-time job with most of the work on the weekend in the fall and winter. Instead of pumping gas, he pumps iron. The towering and impressively hewn Californian resembles one of his home state's majestic redwoods and wears number 77 for the Green Bay Packers.

This special person was born John Spiegel Michels on March 19, 1973, in La Jolla, Ca. A self-proclaimed tall, clumsy and uncoordinated teen only ten years ago, he fought to play on his high school teams. At 6' 4" and 185-pounds, he wasn't necessarily built like the rock of Gibralter. But he did find "The Rock."

While still in his teens, he met with a group called "The Gathering" in La Jolla. One evening he was challenged about his eternal destination.

Specifically, he was asked if he thought he would go to heaven when he died? That night he learned that anything less than a complete trust in Christ wouldn't cut it.

"I accepted Christ as my Lord and Savior right then and there." Friends, John's life has not been the same since. God knew that Michels would choose Him, and He chose an NFL ministry for Michels.

Even with the Lord's help, John needed to work hard. "While the other guys were at the beach, I was in the weight room," he told me. It paid off as John "grew" into his body. After playing only a few years at USC, God ordained him to be the 27th overall pick in the NFL draft. He wasn't drafted to just any team, but to the Green Bay Packers who were on their way to the Super Bowl!

"Big John" is how Reggie White refers to his teammate and neighbor. It was when Reggie White came to John's high school in California for a visit that Michels got really set on fire for God. He became anxious to play with the Packers. When Reggie speaks of Johnny or looks at him, it becomes quite apparent that he is proud of him.

What a joy it was to watch the eyes of the kids at a football camp at Green Bay Community Church when John spoke in June this past off-season. Students hovered all around him, asking for his autograph.

"Yes, but only after we're done. And then I can only sign a few because I don't want to make you late for your next session, okay?"

Reluctantly they agreed that not everyone would get a signature, but each was getting a lesson in people relations that was just as cool.

He proceeded to humbly tell those kids a story about how God honored his dreams and hard work. "You can do the same, but you have to put Jesus first," he said boldly. "If I can do it, you can do it."

I am immensely grateful for the relationship God has given me with John. There is a word that John and I have used often, which I also use in this trilogy. It is Godincidence. I remember preparing to close the door on Leap 1 in April of 1996. I was tempted to include how the Packers had taken Michels and the coincidences that he bore to my other co-host, Ken Ruettgers. I didn't.

My post 1996 draft notes reveal that John, a fellow USC alum like Ruettgers, had been reading Ken's book, Homefield Advantage, at the time he was drafted by the Packers. "Real inspiring," he noted in the Green Bay Press Gazette. If only the parallels between him and Ken would have stopped at both being California natives, left tackles from

USC, big, engaged to be married during their first season and solid born again believers in the saving grace of Jesus Christ, that would have been bizarre enough. But they didn't. It's actually much crazier than anyone could have written in fiction.

The game plan for John was to come in and learn behind Ken Ruettgers how to play left tackle. Then, Ruettgers' left-knee injury changed all that. John was "thrown to the wolves" quickly and responded very well. With Ken's focus needing to be on rehab and trying to get ready to play football, he turned the radio show over to John.

I was impressed the first day I met John at the radio station in September of 1996. He was gracious, friendly and grateful to have an avenue with which to share his faith during the "Timeout" show. As in any relationship, personal or professional, it takes time to get to know one another. We have clicked very well together. John is a down-to-earth kind of guy. I suspect the whole star thing is somewhat uncomfortable for him. He dresses in jeans, a baseball hat and, like me, shaves every other day. You can't help but like somebody like that!

Shortly after we met, John brought Melissa Glenn to the radio program. Their story is one for the romanticists. They met in March, 1996, and when their eyes met, they both knew that was it. They married on February 15, 1997. Melissa recounted the story.

"I went home and called my mom and told her that I had met the man I was going to marry that night. My mom said, 'Don't you think you should date him first?'"

All has worked out quite well.

John and I could never share the same tailor, or pass for twins, but we do have a common bond. We are brothers in Christ, and we have a mutual respect for one another.

John is a prime example of how God honors hard work and commitment. Perhaps God chooses His servants of the Gospel based more on one's availability than the abilities one brings to Him.

Like Ruettgers, because of John's hard work, he need not apologize for being in the NFL. Even John would acknowledge that there are plenty of people in the world who are more talented than he. Most of them are watching, not playing, the games on Sundays. Do you suppose that God knew that a radio co-host for a Christian show was going to be needed in Green Bay? Then a TV show? Or was it about football? Maybe both?

I pay little attention to what John Michels is doing on the field, but he

A little boy's expression toward John Michels says it all. John spoke and gave autographs to a few fans.

has my undivided attention as I see how God has raised him up because of his faith. After being replaced by his friend Ross Verba in the 1997 season after an injury, I was impressed with how he allowed God to continue to refine him and to continue to complete him in Christ. Without question, that was the greatest testimony I witnessed within the Packers in 1997, bar none.

John's job, as he sees it, is to shine the light on Christ. "I play football for one reason. God has given me the ability to play this game for Him. So I do it to the best of my ability for His glory." In a world of overpaid players who appear only to be headed to the beach in a limo, this is very refreshing.

In the "natural," Michels' job as a Packer in 1998 seems still be iffy. I went on record the last radio show of 1997, and continue to take the stand, that God has put a hedge of protection around this man of God because of his faithfulness and his involvement in Christian radio and TV shows.

As I write this, (July of 1998), the jury was still out as John headed for training camp. He could be on the San Diego or New Orleans roster if God wants him there. Or, he could be a gas station attendant back home in LaJolla. I stand by my words, no matter what happens. They will either prove God's "super" on John's "natural" or they will clearly indicate that I should quit prognosticating!

This young man is the deepest-rooted steadfast believer for his age that I have ever met. If you don't agree, read and absorb "The Best of the Leap of Faith Sports Radio Show" chapters in this book. Listen to his profound observations that had even Reggie scrambling at a Bible quiz.

Like his mentor, Ken Ruettgers, who displayed to him the love of Jesus as he came into camp in '96 at the same position, Michels shows that same attitude to his friend, Ross Verba.

"People are like, 'Did you see Ross Verba and John Michels at Hardees?'" he says with a grin. "Yeah, we hang out together. We're great friends. We want the same job, but our bond in Christ supersedes anything as temporal as football." Verba will tell you basically the same thing about his friend.

As Michels headed into training camp for the 1998 season, God blessed him and Melissa with a dose of reality. I called him to see how he was doing on the foreword for this book. Then I asked him if "it" had happened yet.

"Eight pounds and three ounces!" said the proud new papa.

"Congratulations!" We all knew it was going to be a little Lauren Elizabeth, we just didn't know when. I have come to love John Michels for his candor and his willingness to answer any tough question posed to him. His strengths are his honesty and humility. His soft heart became even more so with the birth of his first child.

"Anybody who watches his child being born and still says, 'There's no God,' he said with a pause. "well, I just can't see how they can feel that way. I'm watching this baby come out. She's got my ears and feet and Melissa's hands," he said proudly. "It really puts things into perspective."

John's mind may be more concentrated on family these days, but I have to think he's still not going to take anything from those defensive lineman, and may even give an extra shove for little Lauren Elizabeth. I know that this young lady and any other siblings will be brought up in the love of the Lord. So as not to paint Michels as too perfect, there is one thing about him that is annoying. The Packer coaches have John on this

"Just plain disgusting," is how Steve describes John Michels having to put on weight to satisfy the Packer coaching staff. A jealous Rose looks on.

"enhanced diet" so he will put on weight! That's cruel to the rest of us, eh? Guiltlessly, he sits in the radio studio eating his Big Macs, Frisco burgers and fries in front me knowing full well that the smell alone will mean I'll have to run two extra miles that evening to burn off the excess fat!

Actually, John is, in many ways, just an average guy. He plays his guitar, sings and speaks to numerous youth groups in Wisconsin and California and can often be spotted on his jet ski. But his favorite activity is reading his "love letter" from God, the Bible.

I have come to love John. It's sad the way some of the fans have treated him during the '97 season when he was on the inactive list. My respect rose to a whole new level when he candidly shared how difficult it has been, but that he was trusting in the Lord.

John may not be playing much for the Packers, but he is on God's first team. I have no doubt that John Michels will go down in professional football history as one of the most faithful of all time. I don't know why God has chosen to speak via our media platforms, or why He placed this calling on John's and my life, but I'm so thankful He did.

John and I have coined what has come to be a signature phrase during the show which goes like this. "A hundred years from now, is it going to make any difference whether we won the Super Bowl or not?"

During one radio show last year, I proposed this thought: Maybe God could get more glory by having the Packers lose in the Super Bowl. I cringed then and I cringed even more when I watched it prophetically come to pass on January 25, 1998. John remembered it like a bad dream and phoned me after the devastating loss.

"One of the first things I thought of on the way home, Steve, was how you said God could maybe get more glory if we lost the Super Bowl," he told me. "Let me assure you that what was supposed to happen out there happened." As painful as it was, John remembered that God has a plan.

"God will do whatever it takes to reach people for Him," he said. God's goal is to reconcile Himself to the world through Christ and He'll do whatever it takes to accomplish that even if it means humbling a group of football players." John Michels had the courage to profess it on a network radio and TV show. Maybe, because of it, God will eventually put John in that gas station attendant's uniform.

CHAPTER 8

The Leap of Faith Sports Radio Show 97'

Week #4 • "Rookie, Repeat After Me"

Show #9704   (Recorded Sept. 15, 1997)
Aired on WSRN stations Sept. 19-21, 1997

Steve Rose and John Michels, co-hosts
Ross Verba, guest

From the cozy quarters where we record the "Leap of Faith Sports Radio Show" you could always tell when the guys had arrived by the loud thumps coming down the stairs. Something that used to happen regularly during our first radio season in 1994 occurred on Sept. 15, 1997, as well. In the early years of the program, Ken Ruettgers would bring a Packer guest with him into the studio which created a rather uncomfortable situation for me. The man didn't have a number on him! I'd be wondering, "Who is this guy?" Fortunately, Ken wasted no time introducing the player to me. John did the same here.

With John today was a man I'd never met before. Honestly, I couldn't even begin to guess who he was. His black hat was on backward, he was wearing a huge sweatshirt, and he also was wearing glasses, which is obviously not normal attire on the field.

As per routine, we were seated in the studio and Bob Gardinier, engineer of the show, had all the microphones in place. The guest looked around as if he was in paradise.

"How you doing?" I asked.

"Great. Man, I just think this is so cool that you have a show like this for the Lord. If you ever need anything... time... money or anything, let me know."

I'd only been around the Packer players for three years, but I smiled inwardly wondering if this young man would ever believe in a short period of time what he had said. It appeared he was still basking in the light of autograph seekers, recognition and the newness of being a Green Bay Packer. He almost looked giddy. It felt as if he was more in awe of Bob and me than we were of him. Although that is rather unusual, that is the way I felt.

We were ready to tape. Bob hit the opening for the show and had counted down off the air....three, two, one....go, Steve!

"Welcome to the "Leap of Faith Sports Radio Show," I said enthusiastically. I let the folks know this program is unlike any they've ever heard before, that we report what God is up to inside the greatest conglomerate of born-again Christians today and in the history of professional sports. That may be bold, but it's the truth. My apology to the Vancouver Canucks if, in fact, they have a bigger bunch standing for Jesus.

"John, we do have an important guest. What do you say we bring him in."

"I tell you what, today we have a very special guest. I want to preface this by saying that I invite the guests who are on the show each week. This individual I'm sitting across from right now is someone many people would think I'd be intimidated by because his name is Ross Verba. He was the Packers' number-one draft with the 30th pick in this year's NFL draft...and he just happens to play left tackle."

Of course, what he was trying to say was that it might be considered a bit awkward, maybe even silly, for a left tackle to invite his competition to speak on his radio show. I know John and I weren't surprised. John added that Ross had an amazing testimony to share.

"Ross, welcome to the "Leap of Faith Sports Radio Show."

"Thank you very much, Steve. It's a pleasure to be here."

First on the agenda was to discuss how terrifying it must have been for John just months earlier when, in the draft, the Packers drafter another offensive lineman, particularly with the first pick.

"I was back in Los Angeles and Melissa and I were watching the draft and we're thinkin', 'What's the Pack need this year? Who we gonna go for? Do we need a defensive lineman?'" he recalled. "And then they say, 'With the thirtieth pick in the draft, the Green Bay Packers select Ross Verba, a left tackle out of the University of Iowa!'"

Ross laughed as John explained what was going through his mind in that shocking moment.

"My heart sank. And the first thing I did was pick up the phone and call Ken Ruettgers. 'Ken, is it time for me to start packing? Am I outta here? Are the Packers getting rid of me?' Ken replied, 'John, you know what? You have nothing to fear. I was in the exact same position last year when they said the number one pick was John Michels, a left tackle out of USC!'" Ken knew exactly how John was feeling.

John shared that Ken continued to comfort him during that time. Ruettgers told him, "'John, my greatest fear was that you wouldn't be a good guy.' And you know, I started thinking about that. I told Ken, 'You know, that makes a lot of sense. This guy is gonna be my teammate. He's going to help this team get stronger. Let's just pray that he's a good guy.' And wouldn't you know, God brings another Christian man to this football team in Ross Verba."

John then turned the mic over to Ross to share his powerful story.

"I grew up in the church, but was never really walking with the Lord. For listeners out there, I want to tell you that it's a whole different ball game when you submit your life to Christ. And today, I do have a personal relationship with Him. It's an unbelievable thing."

Verba shared about his college years and how God knew he'd come to Him through football. He talked about going through what he called his "crazy days" at Iowa. In his senior year, with lots of pro scouts knocking at his door, he realized that there was still a major void in his life. Praise God, He filled this hole in Verba. Here's what happened.

"Three days before the draft I opened the door to Christ. And like the Bible says, 'He's standing there waiting to come in.'" (Rev 3:20)

What a thrill and a gift to listen to this new Christian's testimony, and to remember when I accepted Christ into my heart in October of 1991. I couldn't help but smile as Ross told the story.

"And He comes in like a whirlwind."

"Amen," said John very quietly.

"Yeah, amen to that," said Ross acknowledging John's joy in what he'd reported. "I had an emotional experience when the Holy Spirit came in and filled me and from that day forward, it's a whole different ball game, but I'd also like to say it's a process. I'm just a "baby Christian" and a rookie at the same time."

Here's a statement for the ages from this babe who would continue to

Steve clowns with rookie Ross Verba. Verba enjoyed doing the show three times in '97.

tell it like it is. The words which follow never seemed to make it to TV, newspaper or radio, but God means business on the "Leap of Faith Sports Radio Show."

"To be drafted to the Super Bowl champs is one thing, but to be a Christian and have a personal relationship with Jesus Christ just buries the draft."

John could relate, and then took what we heard from Ross to an even deeper and undeniably greater reality.

"The amazing thing about what Ross was just saying reminds me of what I hear from a lot of people. They say things like, 'You know, my life is going real well right now.'" And then somewhat tongue-in-cheek he talked of how many will say, "'I don't need God in my life. Maybe down the road when I'm about to die, then maybe I'll except Jesus Christ.'" I appreciated the powerful way he was able to tie this thought to his teammate and friend's situation.

"What better position could Ross be in? He just finished a great senior year in college. He became a number-one draft pick for a Super Bowl champion team; he's in position to become a millionaire; he could have all the dreams he's had since childhood come true." John paused briefly and, from his heart, ushered a solemn warning. "It's not enough; it's never enough for any of us; it wasn't enough for Ross Verba until he accepted Jesus Christ."

The amazing irony of the Ruettgers, Michels and Verba pattern began to unfold in such an obvious way we had to discuss it.

"Here was Ken Ruettgers who said, 'John, I'm going to take you under my wing. Ken told me the most insecure group of men can be found inside an NFL locker room.'" Both agreed without hesitation as I quickly told the story that very few besides John knew.

"Ken gave John a car to use. Ken and his wife Sheryl had him over for supper and extended themselves in Christian love. Then, I hear that John welcomed Ross with open arms and that you guys did stuff together." It certainly gave me pause for thought. Could I do something for another author or talk-show host coming into my town who might pose a threat to me or my career? Truthfully, I would hope so, but I don't know until it happens. Michels shared a bit of astounding information regarding what has happened in NFL locker rooms.

"You hear story after story of someone who comes into the NFL and the veterans mislead the draft pick to make him stumble so it makes them look better," Michels pointed out. "That was never an issue for me when Ken Ruettgers took me under his wing."

Michels believes his friend's ability to befriend and support him was from more than his own great capacities. "It takes faith. Ken Ruettgers' faith enabled him to be able to accept a first-round draft choice into his home and teach me all the ropes of this game. He taught me how to survive in this game and be good and have success at this level and that stuck with me."

When the opportunity to act in kind knocked with the drafting of Verba, which could have been threatening to John, he responded. "When I was put in the same position, boy, who was I not to follow the example that Ken Ruettgers had shown me?"

"Right," echoed Verba acknowledging that John had done this for him. I felt nudged in my spirit to put into words what I believed Verba was feeling. "I'd be willing to bet, Ross, that this gentleman here did let you know when you came in that he was going to care for you."

"Absolutely, I mean from day one he congratulated me and said, 'It's a pleasure to have you on this team.' I could sense that he was being genuine. It was a great feeling. Then to find out he was a Christian, I knew that he could be a mentor to me as a "baby Christian," not only in football, but off the field, too," confessed the rookie. He also confirmed that Michels had learned well from Ruettgers.

"We spend time together going out to dinner and stuff and we have fellowship. It's really a neat thing for me because I don't know too many people my age in Green Bay that I can fellowship with. It's a nice relief to have that."

We discussed the fact that becoming a born-again Christian is not what we thought it would be. The devil is a liar. He wants us to think that we lose our lives, but Verba, like anyone else who's accepted Christ into his heart, found this not to be the case.

"It puts a whole new spin on life. Once you find Christ, it gives you purpose, it gives you direction, which the majority of the world is looking for. And John can tell you this. As much as we have, it's never enough. When Christ came into my life, it just changed ball games. I was playing this ball game for myself and then I did a total one-eighty. I started living my life for Christ. When you do that, it's unexplainable. It's a miracle," he concluded.

The sweet spirits of these two, big, young men was so touching. John spoke about the Bible, that it is not a book of limitations, but rather that it offers counsel on how to have life abundantly. Ross told of his unquenchable hunger to read the Word of God.

"I can't put it down. I may never finish it; I may never totally understand it; but I'm going try to keep learning more and more." And with a bold authority he proclaimed, "I'll tell you what. For every situation or problem that a person encounters in his life, the answer can be found in the Bible," he professed.

"I'm on my honeymoon with Christ and I want to tell everyone about Him, but in the appropriate manner. I'm so excited about how God has brought us together and I'm excited about what this radio program has to offer," finished the Iowa U star.

We were only two-thirds through the program. Before we concluded, I mentioned that I felt that there were going to be some incredible subplots during the season. There were! One of them had to do with the two men who'd sat in the studio. It brought a whole new revelation to this show and to the situation at large, which changed considerably in the days ahead.

I hugged both behemoths before they left and told them what I tell all the guys. "Thanks for standing up for the Lord." They left together.

No one could ever have imagined the "changing of the guard" which would come the following week. Against the Vikings, while pass blocking Derek Alexander, Michels hurt his right knee. Verba replaced John that day. As of this writing, not only has he not surrendered the position back to Michels, but it would appear that Verba is solidly clamped to the left tackle position.

That afternoon of the taping, none of us could have ever imagined such a drastic shift. This story proved to be one of the Packer stories of the year. Suddenly, the giddy rookie was in the spotlight with John Madden making a fuss over him. Has Verba remained humble? Has Michels found it as easy to continue to help his friend under the current conditions? Has each been able to "walk the talk" of what he discussed during this program despite the shift in their roles? We have some of the exciting answers which are upcoming and just one more leap of faith away.

If you would like a tape of this or any other "Leap of Faith Sports Radio Show", call us at (800) 236-1549.
We would be happy to send you an order blank.

CHAPTER 9

The Packer Hall of Faith

• HOLMGREN'S HALL •

The Packer Hall of Faith
• HOLMGREN'S HALL •

Paul Frase

Born: May 6, 1965
Died:

Green Bay Packers   1997-
#97   Defensive lineman
Syracuse   Drafted Jets, 1988
HT: 6-5   WT: 275

Has played host to a variety of fund raisers to support research for myotubular disease and other congenital myopathies. Co-hosted '96 Holiday Event for Muscular Dystrophy Assn. Active with Fellowship of Christian Athletes.

Inducted into the Packer Hall of Faith as a player in 1998

The name Paul Frase, apart from some divine intervention, will most likely never be in either the NFL or Green Bay Packer Hall of Fame. There is nothing, however, that could keep him out of the Green Bay Packer Hall of Faith. His story of struggle and faithfulness is one for right here and right now.

Paul Frase arrived in Green Bay via the Jacksonville Jaguars. Needing defensive line assistance and a long snapper, the Packers gobbled him up before the '97 season. He's big, well-toned and, according to my female "sources," downright easy on the eyes. Although it's safe to say he is relatively unknown, you may remember the names of a few people with whom he has worked and been friends.

For trivia buffs, Paul was the one who replaced former Jets' star, Mark Gastineau, once he retired. He is great friends with Dennis Byrd, who suffered a tragic injury years ago in New York. None of that will put him in the history books, but that's okay. As with Ken Ruettgers and John Michels, I feel God has taken a man and has honored his faith and hard work.

His journey began as "a PK" (a preacher's kid). At the tender age of eight, he accepted Jesus Christ into his heart to be his Lord and Savior. But according to Frase it really took awhile to sink in...or down, as the case may be.

"Unfortunately, it was eighteen years later when I let God really work in my life," he said. What caused the change?

"Gravity," he told me. Gravity? That's right. "It took eighteen years for the knowledge in my head to sink down into my heart and become a passion for Jesus Christ," he confessed. "Until that time I was not living my life the way I was supposed to."

Today, Paul's and his wife Alison's testimony is in how they deal with their son Joshua's battle with congenital myotubular disease. Their story has impacted many, including yours truly. Because of the care Joshua needs, Paul must leave his family behind in Jacksonville during the season in Green Bay.

Paul spoke at the Pickard Auditorium on "Receivers Night." The sincerity and humility with which he shared his testimony moved me. He is a special man.

Many may remember reading the argument that if the Packers would have had Frase on the active list during the last Super Bowl, we may have come out on top. The Packers didn't suit him up; when Gabe

Paul Frase has one of the truly touching testimonies.
Here he is with Steve and John on the program.

Wilkens went down the line, there wasn't the depth they needed. God, unquestionably, knows what He's doing. It appears to be for something well beyond a need to play football for the Packers that we have been blessed with Paul Frase.

Although he has spent the season alone in Green Bay while Alison and Joshua are back home, Frase does not spend time watching television. Matter of fact, he does not own one!

"I read lots of Christian literature," he said.

He is credited with helping mentor Ross Verba and with hanging out with John Michels to help him, also. Paul's is yet another case where being a professional athlete is no guarantee of being sheltered from the trials and struggles of the world. Ironically, it is because of his trials that he is able to relate to and minister to so many. Paul Frase is another first-round selection in the first year of the Green Bay Packer Hall of Faith.

The Packer Hall of Faith
• HOLMGREN'S HALL •

Kent Johnston

Born: February 21, 1956
Died:

Green Bay Packers   1992-
Began in Tampa Bay 1987
Strength and conditioning
Stephen Austin, Alabama

A graduate of Stephen F. Austin University where he received a bachelor's degree in physical education and history. Secured a master's degree in physical education from Alabama.

Inducted into the Packer Hall of Faith as a coach in 1998

He is one of the most cordial, gentle, impressive personalities inside the Green Bay Packers. The 42-year-old soft-spoken Texan has an impressive walk with Christ. He's a perennial guest on the radio show; his official capacity with the Packers is strength and conditioning coach.

On the field, or should I say off of it, Kent is a mighty presence of importance to all the players. He has been credited with being a real key to the Packers Super Bowl winning season. For the last six years he has played a key role in helping the guys with weight programs, conditioning and nutrition. I recall how he praised two of my favorite people, brothers in Christ.

"At the weekly weigh-ins that I do for the players, Ken Ruettgers and Robert Brooks are the most consistent. They are always nearly a pound from their required weight," he said on the show in 1996. During the breaks, Kent would talk about sharing his faith with his cohorts around the locker room.

Like Pepper Burruss and chaplain Steve Newman, Kent is one of those powerful models of Christ's love and servanthood who is behind the scenes. A well-deserved space in the Packer Hall of Faith is now occupied by this gentle one.

The Packer Hall of Faith
• HOLMGREN'S HALL •

Mike Holmgren

Born: June 15, 1948
Died:

Green Bay Packers   1992-
Began with SF 49ers in 1986
Head Coach   USC

Mike Holmgren Celebrity Golf Tournament has raise approximately $25,000 annually for the Cystic Fibrosis 65 Roses Club. Honorary co-chairman of the 'Harley 100-Mile Run for Muscular Dystrophy'. Also has given time to the Wisconsin Arthritis Foundation telethon. Loves golf and reading.

Inducted into the Packer Hall of Faith as coach in 1998

When the Packers called a press conference in 1992 to announce that they were naming an assistant coach from the 49ers as head coach, it was a real burst of fresh air. We quickly learned about this man of faith and his family. It was encouraging to know that, though the focus was on winning, the main focus of this Godly man was on his Lord and his family.

We documented in Leap 2 that Mike and Kathy Holmgren met at a camp many years ago. After making commitments to Jesus Christ, they have both moved forward in the purpose and calling of their lives. Mike knows that his players would rather see a sermon than to hear one. That is just what he does.

I say, without reservation, that the increased spiritual impact which has been present the last few years in Green Bay did not begin with Reggie White. It began with Mike, a tall and gracious Californian who is being inducted into the most prestigious hall ever. It was he who was able to show the down-to-earth side of Green Bay which lured White here.

The year was 1993, Holmgren's second year in Green Bay. Having read that Reggie White was "waiting to hear from God" as to where to continue his career, Holmgren got an idea. He picked up his telephone and left a very memorable message.

"Reggie, this is God calling....come to Green Bay!"

It was not only memorable, but effective. Because of the call from Holmgren, in addition to the call from the Lord, Reggie became a Packer and the rest is history. What he has already done for the Packers and the community is legendary, but that is not what is most important.

Coach Holmgren lives his life as a Christian in an environment that is not very conducive to do so. He is not perfect and he will tell you that. He is human, but he is covered by the Blood of Jesus Christ.

Case in point. It was Christmas Eve, 1995. The Packers had received a "gift" when Yancy Thigpen of the Steelers dropped a winning touchdown in the end zone. This gave the Packers the Central Division title. Holmgren's postgame speech in the Packer locker room is one inscribed in heaven.

"Folks," he began, "today we received a gift, but let's not forget the gift that God sent in His Son Jesus Christ. Merry Christmas," he said as he walked away. Mike, keep walking right down "Holmgren's Hall" into your chosen place in the Packer Hall of Faith.

The Packer Hall of Faith
• HOLMGREN'S HALL •

Keith Jackson

Born: April 19, 1965
Died:

Green Bay Packers   1995-1996
#88   Tight end
Oklahoma
HT: 6-2   WT: 258

Spent time raising money for P.A.R.K. (Positive Atmosphere for Reaching Kids) in Little Rock, AR. Appeared in the movie "Reggie's Prayer" along with fellow Packer Reggie White. Played cello in high school and college.

Inducted into the Packer Hall of Faith as player in 1998

What I heard about Keith Jackson and what I experienced being with him in 1995 were two different realities. The experience was a pleasant surprise, much as when I had met Ken Ruettgers in 1994. At the time, the media was screaming at us about how selfish and money hungry Keith was when he failed to report to Green Bay after a trade from Miami. Over the next two seasons, we learned the truth.

This born-again believer in Jesus Christ had told the Dolphins he was going to retire to start a Boys Club to help reach youth. It's a shame the Dolphins didn't tell the Packers that when they traded him. Thus, the beginning of the confusion. Of course, I asked Keith about these things after I met him.

"I learned to not fight a battle against the media. You won't win. Why get in a battle with folks who buy ink by the gallon?" he said wisely. His actions over the two years in Green Bay proved to be his defense.

The first thing that hit me about Keith was his enthusiasm and love for life. Ken Ruettgers had brought him in to be a radio show guest and I realized how the media's slant and the real truth about Jackson were diametrically opposed. His sense of humor was fantastic. We'd all be teasing each other. Ken and other players confirmed that he was far from selfish. Jackson's actions after the Super Bowl season showed he was anything but money hungry.

Here are more facts about Keith Jackson. Both Ken Ruettgers and John Michels have said that Keith Jackson has had a tremendous impact as of late in the Packer locker room.

Said Michels, "For me, that first year it was Jesus Christ, family and then Keith Jackson as far as my list of who I thought was great." Pretty strong words from his friend.

From Ken, "Keith Jackson did whatever it took, spending sometimes an hour or more in the locker room, to love people. He'd sit down with people and help them and encourage them."

And the money- grubbing type of comments? False. If Keith Jackson was so money hungry, why did he leave an $800,000 contract on the table to go back to his Little Rock Boys Club called P.A.R.K.? (P.A.R.K. stands for Positive Atmosphere for Reaching Kids.) It is a

From back in 1995 here is Keith Jackson (R)
"hamming it up" with Ken Ruettgers and Steve Rose.

facility borne of a vision from God to care about the young people of Little Rock.

Although his stay in Green Bay was all too brief, his induction into the Packer Hall of Faith is permanent. I can't wait to enjoy some more laughs with him there.

The Packer Hall of Faith
• HOLMGREN'S HALL •

Ryan Longwell

Born: August 16, 1974
Died:

Green Bay Packers   1997-
#8   Kicker
California
Waiver acquisition 1997 (SF)
HT: 6-0   WT: 192

Was a pro baseball prospect. Earned B.A. degree in English. Received the first annual Lee Remmel Sports Award for Professional Achievement in April of 1997. Speaks to youth and church groups about his faith. Has worked with Big Brothers/Sisters and the Special Olympics. Hobbies include playing golf.

Inducted into the Packer Hall of Faith as player in 1998

*Ryan Longwell along with Steve and John during his
debut on the "LOFSRS" in 1997.*

If someone would have said the name Ryan Longwell on the streets
of Green Bay before July 9, 1997, it would have been a miracle if anyone would have even known who he was. On July 9, a Cinderella
story began. After third-round draft choice Brett Conway's injury, the
Packers called on Longwell to fill in. He did admirably, but not without a temporary mountain.

Longwell bolted to the front page at first, not through the thrill of
victory, but the agony of 10-9 defeat. It was a botched 28-yard field
goal against the Eagles that made him a household name. With just
seconds left, Ryan appeared to pull defeat from the jaws of victory.

Longwell, who appeared on the show on the 8th of December, is
easy to love. His youth and size do not make him a dead giveaway to
be a Packer. The truth is, I nearly asked him to leave the studio before
we began recording. I didn't know who he was!

He accepted the Lord as his Savior years ago. Today he walks that
faith as well as any Packer sitting around the table for Bible study.

Matter of fact, it's his faith that has brought him through the rigors of playing in the NFL.

"It's only my faith in Jesus that gives me the peace to kick in this league," he confesses. It was within a split second after the Eagle kick went wide right that God dealt with Longwell. He had made a few and thought the job was going to be easy. Then God made an adjustment in Ryan's thinking.

"In a heartbeat, before the ball hit the ground, I knew God wanted to humble me. He dealt with my pride and I will never take this job or a kick for granted again," he told me.

I had the joy of bringing Ryan Longwell from Madison to Green Bay in May. We had one of the greatest, refreshing talks that I can remember. He, Adam Timmerman, Paul Hornung and I had done an appearance in Madison. I pray that I will have the privilege to do some more. Ryan, welcome to the Hall of Faith.

CHAPTER 10

Reggie: The Packer Rock of All Ages

There will forever be only one Reggie White. He has been larger than life, literally and figuratively, during his tenure in Green Bay. Love him or leave him, he has proven himself to be an outspoken one-of-a-kind in the world of incredibly compensated professional athletes. It would have been safer and easier for the icon to keep quiet and maintain a good reputation. That never crossed White's mind.

For years fans and skeptics alike have rolled their eyes over some of his declarations and proclamations. The numerous physical healings that have left him nothing short of a bonafied medical marvel have brought many believers into the kingdom. It began in 1993 when, fresh off the plane, he said he had received instructions from the Lord to come to Green Bay. He'll admit he was not totally sure why, but that changed after a Super Bowl win.

"I know now why God called me to come to Green Bay," he said after Super Bowl XXXI against the Patriots. "The people here are more open to hear the Gospel of Jesus. Those people who said I was crazy then aren't laughing now. This was all part of God's plan." I'm so glad meeting Reggie was part of God's plan for me.

That meeting with White occurred on November 8, 1994. I, and a few Packers, was backstage at a Racial Reconciliation Rally in Milwaukee. I was flanked by my "bodyguard," Ken Ruettgers, who took me to meet the future Packer and NFL Hall of Famer. Was I nervous as I stood next to White who was seated signing footballs!

"Reggie, this is Steve, the guy I do the radio show with," said Ken before walking away and leaving me with White. My heart was pounding wildly, but then the giant put me at ease.

He stood and extended his hand. "It's nice to finally meet you, Steve. Ken has said a lot of nice things about you," he said in that trademark raspy tone. Like many of the other Packers, he has a gift for making people feel important. Since then White has never done a thing in my presence (or otherwise) which makes me feel anything but admiration and respect for him.

Reggie's first five seasons in Green Bay were relatively smooth. They were filled with accolades and back slaps. However, to say that his off-season after the 1997 campaign has been "interesting" would be like saying there was just "a little panic" during the last hour on the Titanic.

The postseason began in March with a relaxing ten-day trip with Sara and their two children on a "Wisconsin Pilgrimage Tour" to the Holy Lands. A nice-sized group would accompany them as White pondered retirement. Hoping some of the Jordan River would splash on him and heal his aching back, he came back home with the same pain. Then more was on the way. The adventure began with "the speech."

Invited to speak to the state of Wisconsin Assembly, he did just that. It's now a part of history. It appears the legislature thought White would expound on how wonderful it has been playing for the Packers and eating bratwurst. They forgot he is a preacher, first and foremost. He did brag up the good things of Wisconsin, but that's not the part of his meticulously well-planned speech many will remember. In what legislative leaders expected to be only a brief talk, White spoke for nearly an hour.

You see, Reggie White is grieved by the moral decline in America that has reached epidemic proportions. Biblical truths, he believes, will correct the problems. Of course, this notion is not always terribly popular with everyone, especially the media who advocate being "politically correct." Like a sequoia tree, however, Reggie stands strong and unwavering.

During his speech he explained with a variety of examples how different races make up the "complete image of God." It was stuff that's true, but nobody would dare talk about such things. Then, Reggie stepped across a line that no one had dared to cross so boldly. He spoke God's

*From 1996,
Reggie White
towers over
Steve Rose.*

Word which says that homosexuality is a sin. The fur flew! The Bible says in Leviticus 20:13, "If a man lies with a man as one lies with a woman, both of them have committed an abomination." Reggie simply reiterated what God Himself had already said.

With the Assembly now in shock, he told them that he "loved the sinner...but not the sin." Not surprising, that got lost in the transcriptions. Anyone who truly knows Reggie White also knows that he does not hate anyone.

Reggie spoke straight from his heart. White is not concerned about the fans he may have lost or the negative press he's received. He's even less concerned about how many, especially in the media, have chosen to crucify him.

"It's a matter of if I want to be a man of God or not. I'm not worried about my reputation. I'm worried about being faithful to God and His Word," said White to a Green Bay TV personality before the 1998 season. Bottom line? Reggie doesn't care what people think about him.

That's just who Reggie White is and will continue to be. His retirement and unretirement in the course of a couple days in April left many perplexed, but, again, Reggie said he was just being obedient to God.

"After I retired I was having my back rubbed, God spoke to me and told me I made a promise. When I signed a deal last year (1996) I signed a five-year deal with a promise that I would play for two years," said the greatest defensive lineman to ever play the game. He took this word from above very seriously and admitted he really hadn't been working too hard on rehabbing his back.

"God said, 'I want you to fulfill that commitment and the only reason that you don't want to try is because you don't want to work hard to get your back well.'" Sara confirmed it. "I'm a man of my word and of integrity; I don't ever want to back down on a promise," he finished. What's always been clear is that White will do what God wants him to do rather than what's popular.

I'll never forget one of the first things Reggie said when he was on the "Timeout" show with Ken and me. In a world where fans think the players owe them something, White said a single sentence that grabbed my attention. I asked him if it was tough to deal with fans when he and his family were out and about.

"My family is important, and if someone comes up to me during dinner out and bothers me, I may be rude to them," he said seriously. Not a popular stance, but very effective in demonstrating to his wife and kids who's most important to him. As much as White tries to accommodate his fans, the fact is, if there were 92 of him, it still wouldn't be enough.

Dave Koy, from Rothchild, WI., remembers White's talk at a Athletes in Action golf tournament in Green Bay a few years back. Here are Reggie's opening remarks in front of 300 people. They detail even more facts about the man's priorities.

"I'd like to meet each and every one of you tonight, shake your hand and sign autographs," he said. "But I want you to know that there are two kids at home waiting for their daddy to tuck them in and kiss them goodnight. I don't want to disappoint them." That's vintage Reggie.

In Leap 2, you were treated to a glimpse of the real clown that White

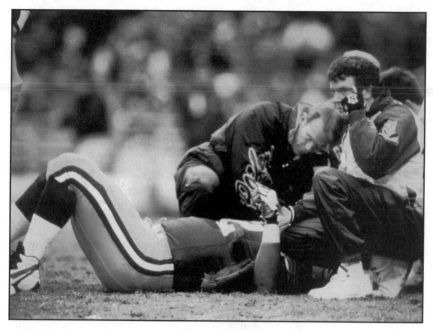

*Pepper Burruss points to his head, which means a
concussion for Reggie White.*

can be. He showed up with Don Beebe at the studio for the Best of the
"Timeout" Show '96 clad in his "Most Valuable Cheesehead" t-shirt. It
was so cool. His deep laughter at Beebe's reminder that their wives were
there to keep them humble was great. I never saw Reggie back on his
heels as he was with Don teasing him. It's the only time I've ever heard
him stammering to fend off the ribbing he was taking.

You will read in "Classic Reggie" (a glimpse of the 1997 "LOFSRS") that
he just gets better with age. That's the beauty of God's economy. As the
body goes, the spirit can be increasing. His comments will make you
laugh and cry. His interpretation of the harsh reality as to why Christ was
crucified will hit you in the chest like a hammer. He's the real deal, folks.
He's in it for God, that's all. He thinks that other Christians need to stop
being so passive.

"I'm tired of the devil pushing us around. God is trying to give people
some guts to speak out about truth." He was asked to debate the homo-

sexuality issue on talk shows and his response was the usual.

"I'm not going to do that because the issue shouldn't be debated," said White. "It's plain and clear what the Word of God says. Jesus didn't debate, so why should Reggie White?"

As I fingered through the variety of pictures I have had taken of Reggie and me, one moment in my memory stands above all the others. I regret that, for a couple hands full of churches in which I spoke, I failed to tell this story that forever defines my image of Reggie White.

It was December, 1994. We had just completed the early morning "Timeout" program. Reggie, Ken Ruettgers and I chatted for just a couple of minutes and then Ken and Reg began to walk to their cars. For some reason, I just stood there and stared at White, in a baseball cap

This poster got lots of attention, including NBC's.

and long black trenchcoat, as he walked to his truck.

I sensed the Holy Spirit was asking me to echo back to Reggie the words he had said to the 4,000 at that Racial Reconciliation Rally the month before. That night he told everyone to bury the racial hatchet, to go and apologize to someone from a different race. We did. As tough as it is for me to admit, I know there is still far too much prejudice toward African Americans in Wisconsin. With White ready to open the door to his vehicle, these words somehow blurted out of me.

"Reggie!" I yelled. He turned and looked at me.

"On behalf of my people (Caucasians) and for myself, forgives us for the racial jokes and the oppression of your people. You know, we really don't know what it's like to be you here in Green Bay."

"Hey," he said somewhat startled and with a little bit of a grin, "It's done already."

He caught me off guard. "It's done already?" I asked myself. Quickly the Spirit of God clarified this for me. God told me this is what he was saying.

"Thanks for the apology, but 2,000 years ago Christ had gone to the cross to forgive me and everyone else for that sin if we'd nailed it to the cross and repented." Reggie seemed to be saying that all of our reactions, African Americans' and Caucasians' alike, have been forgiven if they're under the blood of Christ.

Our eyes locked for a brief moment. I smiled at my brother in Christ. "Thanks Reggie." Then he left.

When people see Reggie White on the field coming around the corner of an offensive lineman towards the quarterback, they see a football player. When I see Reggie White, I hear, "It's done already."

Now, if I would have gone to my computer, pounded that experience out and then sent it to the newspapers, do you think they would have blanketed the front page of the sports section with the following headline?

REGGIE WHITE, MAN OF GOD SAYS, "IT'S DONE ALREADY. CHRIST HAS FORGIVEN ALL SINS FOR THOSE WHO CHOOSE JESUS."

Are you kidding? The evidence seems to suggest that what the media and many fans care about are touchdowns, interceptions, sacks, fumbles, waiver wire transactions and player negotiations. A hundred years from now, will any of those things really matter?

The record shows, and I agree with it, that Reggie White is the greatest, most uncompromising outspoken Christian in the history of professional sports...period. No debate. He doesn't require the approval of man. All that he cares about is whether God is pleased with him. I hope and pray to have the guts to stand as tall and strong as Reggie has. I know it will be easier as I listen to that still voice in my memory which says, "It's done already."

CHAPTER 11

The Leap of Faith Sports Radio Show 97'

Week #5 • "Ken & Pepper"

Show #9705   (Recorded Sept. 23, 1997)
Aired on WSRN stations Sept. 26-28, 1997

Steve Rose and John Michels, co-hosts
Pepper Burruss and Ken Ruettgers, guests

It was another "Who's Who" edition of the radio show. Instead of the usual one-guest format, today we had two guests on the program. Early in the show I acknowledged that Robert Brooks, Don Beebe and Eugene Robinson had been in the studio just two weeks prior, which was not only unheard of as far as quantity, but quality, as well. This week there was John Michels, me and two of the nicest people you would ever want to meet. One guest spent the hour while the other made a "cameo" appearance.

There was a special twinge of excitement for me because one of the guests was a man to whom I feel I owe much of my ministry. He was still "big," in spite of his retirement in 1996. The other guest, a current staffer, is only seen during those unfortunate times when a green and gold warrior gets hurt.

I asked John to bring in the first of our two guests. "I tell you what. I get injured on Sunday and suddenly I have a personal trainer following me constantly to make sure I'm doing alright," he said. "We have Pepper Burruss here who is our team head trainer. He's been here since the Holmgren era began and he is a great man of faith. Pepper, it's great to have you with us today."

"Well, it's great to return to the radio show. It's kind of a yearly event. I was mentioning to Steve we're celebrating my daughter's fourth birthday and the last time I was here we were celebrating her second. It's always fun to come back," he recalled.

It was quite true and equally impressive that he remembered. I can't forget that in 1995, his second time on the show, Ken had encouraged him to leave the studio early in order to get home in time for the party. It doesn't do much good to preach about family if we don't practice it. Today Pepper had a little more time. By the time he left I'm sure the listeners were glad he had stayed as long as he had.

I reminded Pepper that this was his fourth appearance, which was unprecedented in the history of the show. (Steve Newman, the Packer chaplain, would tie him a few weeks later, however.) He reminded me of something funny he had brought up after he was on in 1994. It revealed his gift to chuckle at himself.

"I will entertain you again and say that it just goes to show how low you'll stoop to bring a trainer on to your radio show!" he confessed as we all laughed. I posed a question to the trainer who'd just begun his twenty-first year in the NFL.

"Coincidence or Godincidence that Pepper was there when Dennis Byrd went down in the Jets game? Coincidence or Godincidence that Pepper was around when Reggie White injured that elbow and his hamstring? I believe not," I proclaimed. All of the above happenings had specific evidences of God's touch. We spent time talking about them.

Burruss had described in detail in Leap 1 how Byrd had broken his neck during a 1993 game while Burruss was a trainer with the Jets. He gave an update acknowledging that Dennis miraculously was up, walking, and doing a great deal of speaking. His first bit of wisdom as he recalled this and other miracles on the Packers was this.

"A wise, old mentor of mine said to me, 'God does the healin.' You just do the helpin.' I was in the situation to do the helping and God did the healing because he honored Dennis' tremendous faith."

After a break, I asked John if I could bring in the next guest. It was sort of "old home week." He agreed, but with a stipulation.

"I think I could probably let you do that if I can preface it with something?" he asked. I agreed. "This is a guy who happened to wear my jersey in college." He then hesitated, realizing he had put the cart before the horse. "Well, actually I probably wore his. He came well before me."

Ken Ruettgers had everybody's ears during the "LOFSRS."
Here's John, Pepper Burruss, Ken and Steve.

"We know what you meant, John," I added. Then he started over.

"I wore his jersey in college; played his position in college; went to his same college and I'll leave the rest up to you." As you may have caught on by now, he and I were in the midst of discussing Ken Ruettgers, with whom I'd co-hosted the radio show in 1994 and 1995. He had become a mentor and friend to John in the last couple of years.

"Ken, you don't know how great it is to have you here today," I began.

"Well, it's great to be here and part of this."

I just had to do it; I couldn't help it; I had to digress for just a moment to reminisce about the beginning of this special radio ministry. Back then Ken and I welcomed people like Sterling Sharpe, Mark Brunell and Bryce Paup to the show. It was called "Timeout."

"Wow, 1994. Remember those mornings when we would get in at ten to seven in the morning with toothpicks in our eyes?"

"Yeah, those were early mornings. And the guys showed up," recalled the former offensive lineman with an astonished look on his face. "That was what was even more surprising."

Ken shared that he was now serving as the line coach at West De Pere High School just south of Green Bay, and that he was also involved in an intense Bible study which was demanding about seven to eight hours per week. I asked him how the team he was coaching was doing.

"The team's doing great. We are four-and-oh. Working with high school kids gives me an opportunity to bring a lot of the stuff I've learned on the pro level down and tailor it a little bit for them. It's great fun." Slouched in his chair, he looked over to Michels and gave him this report.

"John, I even give them a test the day before the game like you guys get. Now, I shortened it down so it's not as thick as the test you guys get."

"Do you grade it with the red ink?" asked Michels.

"I don't grade it with the red ink. I thought about that. Then I realized that these are just high school kids and they don't need that kind of pressure," he smiled and laughingly added, "and I don't either!"

I asked him if he motivated with fear by throwing chalkboards and stuff. He confessed that that wasn't really "his style." None of us were surprised. He continued with this point.

"Most of it's encouragement. I think those kids mainly need encouragement. Probably most of them don't get it at home or at school." He admitted that he also knew that after a few weeks as coach the players came to realize that, like them, he has weaknesses, too.

I flashed back with Ken to when he came on the show in October of '96. It was just the two of us. I shared with him how certain I had felt, and that it looked, and I had sensed in his voice, that he was going to be able to play through the pain of his knee. Of course, he couldn't. Romans 8:28 promises that God can use everything for the good of those who love the Lord. Ken had told me both during and after the struggle that good was going to come out of his trial. I reminded him of that.

"You're exactly right. Things do work together for God's glory, but if you look further in Romans you'll find that it's to complete us in Christ. So we do go through trials and we do go through things that we'd rather not go through in order to make us more Christlike."

The reunion of Burruss and Ruettgers in the studio triggered a memory of most prophetic lines in the history of the four-year program. I told everyone it had come from the mouth of Burruss in 1994.

"You're a prophet, Pep," said Ken looking to his right at Burruss. "A modern-day prophet."

"With a non-for-profit job," I said.

"Yeah, a non-for-profit job," complained Pepper facetiously.

"For a non-for-profit organization," added Ken.

Pepper looked a bit bewildered as he explained that we had gotten his attention a minute ago.

"I'm sitting over here with baited breath to hear what I said," mouthed the trainer anxiously. I didn't make him or the listeners wait any longer.

"Well, do you remember when Reggie hurt his elbow in 1994? During the show I looked at you and asked, 'Is Reggie going to be able to play this week against the Cowboys?' You gave this answer, which I reiterated for him now, three years later.

"Well, you know the severity of his injury has been well documented and it looks like he could miss a few weeks." He paused and finished with this. "But you know, knowing where and from whom Reggie White draws his strength, I wouldn't be surprised if he came in tomorrow healed."

Voila! Do you know that is exactly what happened? Burruss told in Leap 1 how White fell into a "divine snooze" during treatment and awoke to find that the Lord had touched him.

"Leave it to Reggie," said Burruss. We spent a short time discussing how the media really never totally "bought" the miracles coming from God over the years. Reggie, Ken, Favre and Brooks all have been met with skepticism when they remark about "divine intervention" for injuries. I asked Ken if he recalled White coming in after this miracle to talk about the frustration from the media. Ruettgers didn't miss a beat.

"People would be more inclined to believe voodoo, crystals or something else like that as opposed to believing in the Lord's strength, and that he (Reggie) had drawn from that."

As long as we were on the issue of healing, I asked Ken about his back injury in 1995. Burruss had shared in 1996 that Ken had defied major odds by rebounding in just two weeks from what would normally have taken nearly eight. I asked Ken what he remembered about it. Little did he know he was about to walk into a trap.

"Yeah, for three or four days I couldn't get out of bed and Sheryl (his wife) had to put my shoes on."

I couldn't resist. "And I bet you kinda enjoyed that, didn't you?"

"It was painful, it was incredibly painful."

Pepper jumped in, reminiscing about how he'd teased Ruettgers on an earlier show.

"Just another long list of things that Sheryl does. Last time I was here I noted that she shovels snow off the driveway; she mows the lawn; now she gets him dressed. She has a special place in my heart. She's a special woman."

"I just married wa-a-a-y over my head," confessed a smiling Ken. "Like most guys do."

We hadn't forgotten about John, who was sitting patiently while listening to Ken, Pepper and me backtrack. I asked him why he thought these things continued to happen in Green Bay.

"You know what? We just have a tremendous group of players here who have faith in God that nothing is beyond God's power. When we take the field, we try to take the field for Him, not for ourselves, and not necessarily for this town's glory." Then, he summed up everything that I have tried to profess and proclaim in these books.

"When men play this game for Him, He is going to respond and be faithful to these men, and He'll be sure that He is glorified through their play and progress on the field."

Twenty-five years old in the natural and about forty-years old in the spiritual - that's how I would describe the Godly intuitiveness of my friend and partner John Michels.

After the next break, it was just Pep and John. Ken returned home to continue work on his Bible study. During the next few moments John showered Pepper with his appreciation for what he had taught him during the second-year lineman's short stay in Green Bay. Listen to what this young man had to say to his trainer.

"One of the really encouraging stories of prayer in my life and the person who encourages me in prayer is actually sitting across from me — Pepper Burruss. I was sitting in the training room last year when all of a sudden his watch started beeping."

John shared that he assumed it was going to be the end of his treatment because Pepper had a lunch date or something. "Why's your watch beeping? And he says 'Well, this is my reminder that it's time for me to pray,'" he recalled humbly.

Burruss was quick to confess that while it's true that he sets his alarm for this purpose, the challenge to do so had come from another special man inside the "God Squad" about whom few hear.

"Steve Newman, who does our chapels as the team chaplain, issued that challenge. Now, you kind of convict me," said Burruss to Michels, "because with this new watch I've been given to try out, I have to reset the alarm." The watch was black and huge, really huge! John would have some fun with this in a few minutes.

The head trainer also took this as an opportunity to reach out to the listeners for help. He noted that the team was "awfully banged up" and could use all the prayer they could get. Interestingly, he shared that the team prays for the safety of both teams before every game.

"We place no value in someone on the other team getting hurt. We don't want to see the game change because someone is getting hurt--a star or not. Sadly, injuries are a part of this game so please pray for all of us. It's a great feeling to know that it's a toll- free phone call to God."

"And, a local one from Green Bay," I added.

I then started a little conversation which I was sure would lead to some teasing. I looked at Michels and began.

"John, I don't want to hit a nerve here, but Pepper talked about people sending him stuff to try out, like the watch. He gets paid "big bucks" for that." I recalled what Burruss had said a couple years ago about wishing he could wear some apparel on the sidelines that would help line his pocketbook. He took the bait.

In his best Italiano voice, he jokingly mumbled, "Like Rocky. Hey, Mick says I should wear this. I get the jacket, he gets three grand!"

Michels couldn't resist jumping in and commenting on Pepper's watch. "You gotta see this watch, too. This is a watch for the blind." (I lost it at this point!) "I mean, I can see it from across the field. You know, I could be sitting there in the huddle and say, 'Hey Pep, what time is it?' and all he would have to do is hold up his wrist and I'd be able to tell what time it is."

The crafty helper for healin' never missed a beat as he stared at Michels and noted, "You know I'm in such a mood to say, 'When my alarm goes off it means, John, it's time for you to block the guy across from you.'"

"Oooohhh," I groaned for my big buddy. Every once in a blue moon we have zingers on the program and that was definitely a zinger.

"Talk about persecution on the show," lamented John.

"Pepper, we have to pray for forgiveness for you," I teased.

We touched on Brett's ankle injury in '95 where he was divinely touched. We spoke also about Reggie's hamstring and Brooks' knee recovery. He made what I thought was a great observation about the players who'd been injured and then touched by the Lord.

"Definitively what was touched and easy to see in the training room was their spirit. Their pain was healed. They were touched in such a way that they were able to deal with the situation with which they were faced." He wasn't through.

"Reggie still, to this day, has a noticeable defect in the muscle in his hamstring yet functions fully in spite of it. And Robert's deal is such testament to his faith and hard work."

It was time to go. We thanked Pepper for coming in and I teased John about being from La Jolla, (pronounced LaHoya) California.

"We were close to Tijuana, Mexico," he said.

"Did you speak Spanish?" I quizzed.

"Not really, but many of the people out there are bilingual."

"Doesn't that mean you can throw a football with both arms?" I asked.

John laughed. I suspect our faithful audience just groaned. It was a good way to close. After all, it had been that kind of program.

_____

If you would like a tape of this or any other
"Leap of Faith Sports Radio Show", call us at (800) 236-1549.
We would be happy to send you an order blank.

CHAPTER 12

Packer Power

I've said it once. I'll say it again. "This Packer thing is just crazy." As a rule, the further away you get from Green Bay the crazier it gets. Since the release of <u>Leap of Faith: God Must Be A Packer Fan</u> in September of 1996, it's felt like we've circled the globe a couple of times.

In my travels via air or ground, the further away that I get from my home in Neenah, the more I realize how many people have never even seen a Packer. It's also apparent just how powerfully the fans are affected by the players. I know because they share this with me.

My mailbox is full of letters from people who remind me how fortunate I am to have the joy of spending time around quality men of character and integrity, who just happen to be football players. They're right. The phone rings constantly. I'm glad I talked Kim out of changing our phone number. It rang last February with details of one of the greatest fan/Packer stories ever.

"Hi, is this the Steve Rose who wrote Leap of Faith?"

"Yes it is," I said.

The lady on the other end went on to tell me that her name was Gretchen from Superior, Wi. I've never been there, but I know it's coooold there in the winter. She told me about her brother, Michael, who was a Brett Favre fan. Michael was dying from cancer.

She explained to me, "Michael read in Leap 2 about Robert Brooks' miracle (Chapter 5--Rise and Walk Again) and that it was his faith which brought him through. Now he wants to talk to Robert Brooks. He realizes that there isn't anything Brett could tell him." This isn't a knock on Brett. It's just that when we cut to the chase of life and death, all that matters is Jesus. I would hear from Gretchen later.

I got a great letter on January 18, 1998, from a wonderful lady in Francis Creek, Wi., by the name of Sister St. Francis. Her letter started out with a bang.

Dear Steve,

I AM A PACKER FAN! besides being a Catholic Nun. (That comes first.) She went on to explain she had received Leap 1 for Christmas in 1996 and Leap 2 in '97. The first was being circulated with "spilled chocolate on it."

Steve Rose signs an autograph for a Packer fan at Waterloo High School.

Steve Rose with many of the many Packer faithful at a book signing.

She said, "I can't begin to tell you how edified I am and inspired by the work you, Ken Ruettgers, John Michels and all the Packers are doing for Christ."

She went on, "No wonder God is a Packer fan! It is amazing in this day and age that there are such wonderful Christians including Reggie White who are evangelizing the world, bringing all to accept Jesus as Lord and Savior."

On February 24, I was invited to speak at St. Anne's School in Francis Creek. Shortly after, my new friend blessed me once more when she wrote this to me after my speaking engagement with them.

Dear Steve,

I am still on "cloud 9!" Your presence here at Francis Creek on February 24th was one of the highlights of my entire life. I shall cherish your visit forever.

Thanks for autographing my books. Listen to this. Whenever a sister dies, and is laid out for viewing, several of her personal memorabilia are put on display. Today I told one of the Sisters, "When I die I want my two books to be placed on display, open to Steve's autographs."

My sister in Christ, I give God the glory for your reception of the message of salvation and for affirming to me that God has called this group of men in green and gold to Him. It's that simple.

I am going to try, God willing, to put Sister St. Francis on the TV show this coming year.

On March 28, through the efforts of Sharon Woodall, a Godly sister in Christ, I was privileged to speak in West Bend at a benefit for Sherri Zagar from Richfield, Wi. Her life hangs in the balance as of this writing unless she receives a complicated bone marrow match. I was so moved by Sherri's faith. Though her life could end, she is not afraid.

"If I'm here, great. God has more work for me. If not, I'll be home with Him," she told me. Hats off to her husband, Peter, who is just as strong in the fight. You see, Sherri Zagar has trusted Jesus Christ as her Lord and Savior and has a peace about her life. Love and peace radiate from her. Sherri, thanks for showing me the love of Jesus.

On May 30, I had the joy of making a trip with my friend Brad Vivoda. The destination on the "Leap of Faith Book Tour" this day was Cedar Rapids, Iowa. It was there that I learned a great deal from a teacher and Packer fan extraordinaire by the name of Mike Trosky. He told me how Ken Ruettgers' book had challenged him to become an even better dad. I spoke to the students at Prairie Middle School and a FCA group. Both were great opportunities and, again, I got to experience the love of Jesus Christ from my encounters.

I shared the story about how Kim had lost her whole family in a plane crash in Iowa years ago. I will use the story at times to emphasize the preciousness of life. I was touched that a girl wrote to Kim on a business card.

Mrs. Rose,

I thank you for blessing me with your husband's talk and hope you also know your story is a blessing to me. God bless.

Nicole Snyder
Cedar Rapids, IA

On June 28, I spoke at the First Presbyterian Church in Oconto. Many came to accept the Lord Jesus Christ on that day inspired by the Packer testimonies and my story of a fool in the first degree. It appeared, however, that we were called to minister in a very special way to Ann Freiss.

Steve and his "favorite fan", Sister St. Francis.
"She is so sweet," says Steve of his friend.

To God goes all the glory for this one, too.

A few years ago, she was diagnosed with cancer and given only four months to live. She even went with her mother to pick out a casket. However, after one of Reggie's many miracles, Ann took her own leap of faith to call on the same Power that healed Reggie to now heal her. Today she is cancer free!

She is healed, praise the Lord! She told me, "I believe you were sent to me today to share again how Reggie White's faith helped me make a choice, too. Reggie's testimony is helping many others." I passed along a letter from her to the big man.

Nothing has been more sobering than a call I received at 12:40 in the morning just recently! A sobbing woman named Laura told that Leap 1 had helped her exercise faith to beat cancer. Though she still struggles in her faith and life, Laura credits reading about Robert Brooks in Leap 1 as what enabled her to call on God in a leap of faith to heal her, as well. She is a special sister in the Lord.

What a privilege it has been to have been entrusted with the gospel which can bring help and healing to peoples' lives. I consider it a joy to be God's servant.

It was at the beginning of June when the Lord put Michael from Superior on my heart and in my mind. I called Gretchen. She was not in her office.

I went to the post office a few hours later. There was a letter from Gretchen! She told me that Michael had had a streak where it seemed he was healed. Reggie had called him and told him he would have a great testimony someday. That he has.

Shortly after the time it seemed that Michael was healed, his cancer returned. On May 15, 1998, Michael died. God chooses, in some cases, to call his sheep home. We don't understand why some are healed and others are not. I had told Gretchen months before that, as unfortunate as it is, sometimes it takes a funeral to wake people up and to show the power of hope when a Christian dies. That's just what happened.

You see, Michael Stariha knew Jesus Christ as his Lord and Savior. The Bible promised that he would go to heaven when he died. We, who are in Christ, will get a chance to meet Michael. (The closest he had been before that to heaven was Lambeau Field on September 21 last year when we beat the Vikings!)

I pray these true life and death stories have reached you and have reminded you once again that all that should and will matter is what you have done about God's Son, Jesus. Are your sins covered by the blood of Jesus?

Now, a little surprise. It is with great Packer power and pleasure that we induct Michael Scott Stariha into the "fan wing" of the Packer Hall of Faith! He shall be the first fan inducted there. Later, you can join him. (See "The Last Chapter of #66.") It's great to know that when I get to heaven I'll know Michael by his Packer jersey. And Michael will know me. I'll be the one carrying a couple of books and, oh yeah, there will probably be a pretty groovy nun with me.

CHAPTER 13

The Packer Hall of Faith

• NITSCHKE WAY •

The Packer Hall of Faith
• NITSCHKE WAY •

Mike McCoy

Born: September 6, 1948
Died:

Green Bay Packers   1970-1976
#76   Defensive tackle
Notre Dame
Drafted by GB 1st rd
HT: 6-5   WT: 285

Has worked for Campus Crusade for Christ for many years. Speaks to thousand of individuals sharing his faith every year.

Inducted into the Packer Hall of Faith as player in 1998

The NFL and Packer diehards remember that the Packers took Mike McCoy with the very second pick in the draft in 1970. The only player taken before him was Pittsburgh Steeler great Terry Bradshaw. A consensus All-American at Notre Dame, he started with the Packers his rookie year for coach Phil Bengston and then played for Dan Devine.

The popular McCoy toiled on the field and made a great impact for seven seasons in Green Bay, but his greatest impression was on the fans and his teammates during what McCoy told me were B.M. days.

"I played 'before money,' laughed McCoy recently. "Back then there wasn't the money that is in the game today." The $700 a month he collects in pension today is not comparable to the benefit package he received in 1971 from above.

"During 1971, God's truth captured me and I accepted Christ as my personal Savior. I was very spiritual as a youngster, but still felt an emptiness." Jesus filled that God-sized whole in McCoy.

"I had gone to Notre Dame and had taken philosophy, but I didn't get it. I thought if you were good, you could get to heaven." he recalls. "It's not about religion, or going to church. It's about a personal relationship with Jesus Christ."

He credits former Packer Carroll Dale, who led Bible studies for the Packers, with helping him in his walk with the Lord. Around the league he tips his hat to people over the years in the NFL like Bill Glass, Raymond Berry and Tom Landry. He credits current Packer chaplain Steve Newman with helping to nourish the Christians on the Packers beginning in 1975.

In 1974, when the Packer Report magazine came out, his tiny daughter Molly was asked, "Why is your daddy a good player?"

"Because my daddy loves Jesus!" was her answer. That he does and today he spends his time exalting Jesus Christ.

Fellow Hall of Faith recipient Ken Ellis thanks McCoy for helping him find Christ. He presented Ellis into the Packer Hall of Fame on March 14, 1998. Now, it is with great honor that Mike McCoy takes the place which has been reserved for him since the beginning of the world in the Packer Hall of Faith.

The Packer Hall of Faith
• NITSCHKE WAY •

Steve Newman

Born: April 24, 1948
Died:

Green Bay Packers   1975-
Chaplain

Escorts and interviews numerous Christians on the
Packers before large crowds during the off-season. Works
for Campus Crusade for Christ as well as serving with the
Packers. Enjoys spending time with his family.

Inducted into the Packer Hall of Faith as a chaplain in 1998

★   ★   ★   ★   ★   ★   ★

It was 1994 when I met the man the guys call "Newms." Tall, slender
and blonde, Steve is without a doubt a major driving force behind the
power the Holy Spirit has blown through Green Bay. His twenty-one
years as chaplain with the green and gold have packed a wallop according to the men he serves. What does the chaplain do?

"I look at my role as that of a shepherd. I look at my responsibility from
the Lord as a calling. My job is to help the players to become the best that
they can be, but also to help them deal with reality," he said during his
'97 visit on the radio show. "Once a person places his trust in Christ, he
is able to look at things from a different perspective."

One of the things you may see Newman doing on TV is carrying the electrical cords for Fritz Shurmur, the offensive coordinator. Newman's job and prayer each game is to protect Shurmur. Steve is one of few who has a chance to watch the incredible emotion that goes on from the sidelines each game, as well.

Professional football players are some of the most insecure people on the face of the earth. Steve is there to help them keep the focus where it needs to be kept. Do you think it's easy to minister to a Super Bowl caliber squad? It may not be what you think. Former Packer Ken Ruettgers has learned to appreciate Newman as much as anyone.

"The fact of the matter is, it's a tough job for Steve dealing with a group of guys who are experiencing success," said Ken. "Blessing can take our focus off the Lord; Steve is someone who can help keep the balance, but it's a battle." Newman just wants everything for the players that God wants for them.

"I want to help anchor the players to become the best they can be in Christ. Fellowship, God's Word and emotional cleansing is a huge part of what I try to do with the guys." John Michels has learned to appreciate Steve, too.

"He challenges us each week to be the best we can be, not for ourselves, not for the fans, not for financial success, but for the kingdom of heaven," said the second-year pro. "There is a security knowing that he is there with us on the road."

During the Detroit game in '97, when Beebe and Michels went down, Ross Verba approached Newman with a question.

"Are you praying?" he wondered.

"Can you see my eyes?" he asked the rookie.

Ross saw the tears and no other explanation was needed.

I hope you have had or will have the opportunity to meet this gentle, humble man who loves the Lord with all his heart. I want to be more like Steve Newman. Brother, take your place now for eternity in the Green Bay Packer Hall of Faith.

The Packer Hall of Faith
• NITSCHKE WAY •

Ray Nitschke

Born: December 29, 1936
Died: March 8, 1998

Green Bay Packers   1958-1972
#66   Linebacker
Illinois
Drafted by GB third rd
HT: 6-3   WT: 225

Was involved in numerous charities including a variety of telethons. Was a spokesperson for Right to Life groups. Had a practice field named after him behind the Don Hutson Center. Inducted into the Wisconsin Athletic Hall of Fame.

Inducted into the Packer Hall of Fame as player in 1978

Inducted into the Packer Hall of Faith as player in 1998

I believe it is simply the greatest story in the history of the Green Bay Packers. It's the Ray Nitschke story. Many may think it's about an orphan who makes it big in the NFL, but there is so much more to it than that.

Ray is the only member of the Hall of Faith who is now being inducted posthumously. His legend as the greatest middle linebacker to ever play the game will live on. His thick black-rimmed glasses, bald head and duck-footed walk on the field will forever be etched in fans' minds.

Please allow me to portray the induction of Nitschke into the Hall of Faith as a kind of cake. The frosting is coming in the last chapter of this book, "The Last Chapter of #66." You will read a story so touching, so loaded with God's divine timing, that you will never forget it, I'm sure.

His ability to go from a madman to a pussycat was baffling. His ability to entertain with a kind, quiet demeanor was known by too few. Carroll Dale, his roommate for his last eight years in Green Bay, remembers Ray this way.

"He was like a raving madman on the field and a teddy bear off of it," he said. Quite a contrast, yet so true. There was a reason Ray took out a lot of anger on the field and why he became so sweet the last few years of his life on earth. The "mystery" will be exposed in the later chapter.

Nitschke never failed to sign an autograph, ever. He traveled frequently to do things like play on the Packer traveling basketball team. He loved to entertain people by shooting hook shots from half court. He never hit the backboard, but they cheered as he shot those hooks!

Today, Ray Nitschke is in heaven and in the Packer Hall of Faith based on the acceptance of a promise. It's not because he was a great husband, father and football player; not because he's in the NFL and Packer Hall of Fame; it's because of a promise. What is it? Details are coming.

It breaks my heart that Nitschke will never be able to come to any Hall of Faith ceremony here on this earth, but born-again believers will see Raymond again, oh yes! In the meantime, Ray, enjoy your stay in the Packer Hall of Faith and God's Hall of Faith called heaven.

The Packer Hall of Faith
• NITSCHKE WAY •

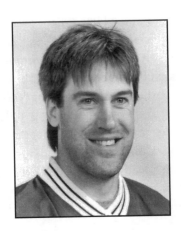

Doug Pederson

Born: January 31, 1968
Died:

Green Bay Packers   1995-
#18   Quarterback
Northeast Louisiana
Free agent 1995
HT: 6-3   WT: 216

Shares his testimony of faith to audiences. Has worked with the Cerebral Palsy telethon in Louisiana. Volunteers his time to speak in schools in the off-season. Enjoys water activities and golf.

Inducted into the Packer Hall of Faith as player in 1998

Doug Pederson, like Ryan Longwell, hasn't become a familiar name in the homes and hearts of all Packer fans, but he has in God's kingdom. His muscular frame is contrasted by his soft-spoken voice. The back-up quarterback to Brett Favre was gracious enough to make a visit to the "LOFSRS" in 1997 to tell us about himself.

"I grew up in a Christian home in a small community called Ferndale, Washington. I accepted Jesus Christ at Vacation Bible School. Both my parents taught and they led me to the Lord," he recalled. "Ever since, I've just been blessed with God's grace upon my life."

Pederson, number 18 with the Packers, was in Miami in 1993. He led the Dolphins to Don Shula's 325th win. His arrival in Green Bay hasn't come with much travail or trial.

"I was cut six times by Miami and Carolina. I felt like my career was over. My faith was tested. It was then I realized that I had to give my circumstances to God. He works in mysterious ways; to Him be the glory." Amen.

He went on to explain and reemphasize, just as John Michels has done many times, that he is in the league playing for the Packers for one reason, which is to raise up the name of Jesus Christ. God is the one who has put him in the NFL and he wants to give the blessing back to Him to further the kingdom.

Pederson thanks Steve Newman for the time he has given him to help him grow in Christ. He also has a special place in his heart for former roommate and now retired Don Beebe.

Doug Pederson is another name that certainly won't make it into the Packer Hall of Fame, but it is one that simply cannot be prevented from entering the Packer Hall of Faith. Doug, "Well done, thou good and faithful servant."

The Packer Hall of Faith
• NITSCHKE WAY •

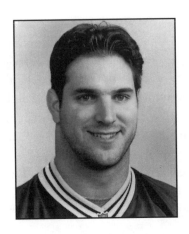

John Michels

Born: March 19, 1973
Died:

Green Bay Packers   1996-
#77   Offensive tackle
USC
Drafted by GB in 1st rd
HT: 6-7   WT: 300

Speaks to various groups and organizations about his faith. Has done a Christian show called "The Leap of Faith Sports Radio Show." Has served Athletes in Action and Fellowship of Christian Athletes. Loves jet skiing, golf and playing guitar. Earned a B.A. degree in religion.

Inducted into the Packer Hall of Faith as player in 1998

Please allow me the liberty to present my co-host and trusted friend into the Green Bay Packer Hall of Faith. When I think of John Michels, I think of a big man. Not only is he big as far as size, but he's a man who is big in the eyes of the Lord. At 6-7 and 300 lbs., he is currently the tallest player for the Packers. He is one of the greatest physical specimens walking the Green Bay facilities, but those are not the most impressive things about John Michels.

As you have been able to tell by now, this 25-year old is well beyond just football. He is deep in his love for his wife and his family, but most of all for his Lord and Savior, Jesus Christ. He met the Lord in a powerful way after attending "The Gathering" in La Jolla, California. His life has not been the same since.

Quite frankly, since John has come to Green Bay as a first-round pick in 1996, he has had quite a roller coaster ride. After playing upon arrival after Ken Ruettgers' retirement, 1997 found him bamboozled by what was happening. So was I. Ross Verba, his friend, wound up with his job and Michels would find himself, during the latter part of the season, on the inactive list in street clothes. Why such a nightmare for such a faithful person? All I know is John is a better person today because of it.

Without a lot of hard work, it would have been virtually impossible for John to make it to the NFL. He does not take his position or call from God lightly. He has worked as hard as anyone. I believe his heart for God is what has given him the platform that he has. As my partner for the past two years with the radio show (and now a TV show), we both have a passion to share the Gospel of Christ.

His talents are many. From playing the guitar to writing the foreword for this book, he is definitely a multi-dimensional guy. Sweet, generous and kind are just a few of the words which come to mind when I think of John Michels...a regular kind of guy.

No matter what the future holds for John, I will never forget that he stepped in, at the expense of his own time, to help me continue this ministry in 1997 when the fire was nearly out. Because of him, there is not only a radio network, but this book, and now a TV show which will be the first of its kind anywhere.

John, you will always be a first-teamer in my heart. I thank you for all you have done for me and for the Lord and His Kingdom. So now, proceed to your well-deserved place in the Packer Hall of Faith. It looks like Ken Ruettgers is there waiting for you.

CHAPTER 14

The Greatest Leaper of All

He's one of a kind. One word describes him better than any other...class. His friends call him 'Shoo-in.' You know him as Robert Brooks. Love oozes from him when you simply stand in his presence for any length of time. It became even more obvious when he became a national spokesperson and ambassador for the Packers. It really started on September 15, 1997.

"It was that day when I scored a touchdown against the Giants," he vividly recalls. "I decided I was going to do something to take peoples' minds off Sterling Sharpe for just ten seconds," he told us. It's history. It's called the "Lambeau Leap." More than the points that are put up on the board, it's awesome to watch the grace and the glide of this role-model rocket.

Thrown into the Packer mix as the go-to-guy in 1995 after the retirement of Sterling Sharpe, Robert has produced on the field. Despite the career threatening setback with his knee injury, his time away was short. Brooks has come back on the scene as strong as ever. These days Brooks plays the game of football for all of the opportunities it provides. He's bold with his testimony and, like Reggie White, is not concerned what people think of him.

How many people do you know who are courageous enough to admit that God has spoken to them? Other than Reggie, it's not exactly the norm in professional sports. When we say that God spoke to Brooks, we are not saying God showed up at the front door of his home. What Robert did feel was a penetrating message which was inscribed on his heart. It was emblazoned there just a few weeks into the 1996 season, according to Brooks.

On the 1997 "Leap of Faith Sports Radio Show" Robert reiterated what had taken place a year earlier. "God showed me that I would not be finishing the season. It didn't scare me or anything. He literally showed me about a year and a half of my life," he remembered. "I saw myself going through something; I didn't know at the time what specifically it would be, but I also saw myself coming out the other side stronger in my faith."

The eight-year Packer veteran took a deep-rooted leap of faith to believe God rather than man, which isn't always easy. The choices were only

Steve "cracks Robert up" during one of their public appearances together promoting Leap of Faith 1 and 2. Rose's inspiration and brother, Gary, is at right.

two: believe the doctors who told him he'd 'be lucky if he could walk without pain and a hitch,' much less play football again; or to trust God who had implanted in his heart the belief that He was going to restore him physically and take him to a new plateau in his faith.

Because he's human, and because of the track records and terrible odds of such a recovery, we would have understood if Robert had bought into the medical personnel's prognosis rather than God's. Robert believed God. Since his recovery, both Brooks and the world he touches are changed by his experience.

John Michels said recently, "Robert is just on fire! He is a great leader and loves to share how good the Lord has been to him."

Ken Ruettgers, who is deeply respected by Brooks, points out that, "Robert Brooks loves God and is wisely using his powerful platform as a Packer. He is maximizing the opportunity he has to reach people with God's goodness and to tell them you don't have to be a football player to be touched by Jesus."

It is difficult to describe the power I felt as I sat with Brooks in his Green Bay home that July day last year. I will never forget how he started out a bit tired; then just began to fire up under an anointing. That story eventually turned out to be one of the highlights in Leap 2, "Rise and Jump Again." God led Brooks through a remarkable series of miracles. Today he continues to flow in the anointing and shares more than ever before that God can do so much more than we ever imagine (Eph 3:20) if we will just believe.

During the last off-season, Robert was speaking at the Pickard Auditorium in Neenah along with teammates Paul Frase and Doug Pederson. As Brooks shared his testimony to the estimated 800 strong, he lovingly "jabbed" me with a reminder of how I had teased him during a recording session at his home last summer.

"Steve Rose looked at me and asked my brother, 'Should we get the people in the white coats to take your brother away?'" I acknowledge that I did say that to his brother, Charlie. I was having some fun with him. Brooks certainly wasn't crazy then and, for those of you who still might be skeptical, he isn't now, either.

In the second season of his comeback, Brooks is poised to be even

Steve and Robert relax in Brooks' Green Bay home.

stronger in the 1998 Packer campaign than last year's. What's most impressive, however, is the strength that he carries through his faith. Time and time again I meet individuals who have found strength and encouragement from the story of how God took a lukewarm faith and turned up the heat.

Not only is Brooks enjoying a deepening walk with Jesus, but lives continue to be affected within the Packer faithful numbers. You will read one such story in "Packer Power." It's a story which is of eternal value.

"People ask me, 'Weren't you mad that you were hurt for the first Super Bowl,' and I say, 'No.' Look at what God has done in my life. Look how He is being glorified through this situation."

I can personally attest to the fact that Robert felt certain something great was going to transpire as a result of his injury. He trusted what the Lord had told him and it proved to be accurate.

Robert Brooks will go down in the history of the Packers as not only the most huggable creature to fly and land into the front rows of Lambeau Field, but one of its most dedicated, tireless, and disciplined workers. His

Robert Brooks gives Steve Rose "rabbit ears" after the 1996 Leap of Faith press conference. Rose had "no clue" why everyone was laughing.

three-percent body fat is a testimony to his discipline. He always has the steamer cooking something, and he drinks those protein drinks mixed with vegetables from the blender. What pours out of it looks like something on a late-night horror show, but it works!

The Bible says physical exercise is good, but spiritual exercise is even more important. Robert has a Bible with him constantly, whether he's on the plane or hanging out at home. He can be seen holding his Bible on computer in a Leap 2 picture where he and I are pointing to his born-again knee.

Brooks' number-one commitment is to Jesus Christ. On November 4, 1997, Robert Brooks made another commitment. It is to be a great husband. He and his wife Diana are expecting their first child. To get a new and fresh start, they have moved to a new home. Teammate Gilbert Brown now enjoys the former Brooks' homestead where Robert had spent a great many hours in prayer.

It would be great to see Robert Brooks in a Green Bay Packer uniform for many years to come, but the reality is he, like any one of his teammates in the league, is always a possible one-play away from a wheelchair. We have all watched Robert take hits from cornerbacks that would knock normal people into oblivion. He had no less than two concussions in the first four weeks of the 1996 season. He is not to be taken for granted for what he is doing on the field or off it. He's a fighter and will not back down. He refuses to quit. That's especially true when it comes to his faith.

"If you come to my house, you're going to hear about Jesus," he once told me. "I'm going to surround myself with Godly people so I can protect myself from the enemy." As a regular in the accountability group and the Bible studies inside the team, let me assure you that this is exactly what he is doing.

I hope those hometown natives of Greenwood, South Carolina, are proud of their boy. We sure are. After all, how many people do you know about whom there has never been a bad word said? I can safely say Robert Brooks, without question or hesitation, is one of those rare people. I'm not talking about the knocks he has taken about being too small or being injury prone. I'm referring to his character and his integrity, the true man who lives inside the twenty-eight year old body.

It has been great to spend time with Brooks. We linked up in 1996. At a July press conference Brooks announced he was releasing his song "Jump," and I announced the publication of Leap 1. After we addressed the media, the slender one turned to look at the color 5 x 7 foot replica of the book's front cover which showed him leaping into the stands.

"This is gonna be great," he beamed.

"Yes, I know," I said.

It has been, but little did we know what road Brooks would have to go down in order to achieve a place on the narrow path to greatness in Green Bay. It's been a bumpy one. Still, Robert has no regrets. Because of the strength he gained through it, his leap of faith and his leap into the stands are higher than ever.

CHAPTER 15

The Leap of Faith Sports Radio Show 97'

Week #11 • "Classic Reggie"

Show #9711   (Recorded Nov. 3, 1997)
Aired on WSRN stations Nov. 5-7, 1997

Steve Rose and John Michels, co-hosts
Reggie White, guest

In walked "the man" in a green and gold button-down Packer shirt which was cut like a baseball jersey. Wearing green denim pants and tennis shoes, he looked much slimmer than the last time I'd seen him. He was. It's always a treat to spend time with the man who has been called the "minister of defense" around the league and in Green Bay. Many know him just as Reggie.

For the third time in the four-year history of the program, we were able to encourage Reggie White to come in to spend some time with us. He appreciates the safety of the show. There's no mob around, and he is free to share what God is doing in his life without anyone looking at him as if he had three arms.

Bob Gardinier had yet to meet Reggie so I introduced them. Bob's son, Andy, who is 10, had accompanied his dad to work that day. I'm sure he must have thought he'd won the lottery to be in White's presence, if only for an hour. He calmly sat next to White for most of the show.

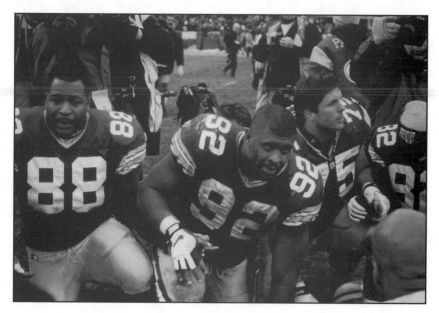

Keith Jackson, Reggie White and Ken Ruettgers.
"Where is the fifty yard line of your life?" Ken once asked a fan.

Also in studio was my friend, Rev. Kevin Penniman, who is a pastor and a pilot. "Rev. Kev" (as Ross Verba and I call him) is from Rockford, Illinois. He may be from Illinois, but he's "normal" in that he is a Packer fan. Kev was in town to fly Ross Verba and me to western Wisconsin the following day.

As the show started, I immediately mentioned that Reggie was there, and then asked John what he'd been doing recently. He had taken the prior week off to vacation. The Packers had played the previous Monday against the Vikings. Monday is when we normally tape. I was glad to know he had been thinking about us.

"I missed you last week. With the time off, I managed to get away with Melissa."

"That family thing is okay," I told him.

"Family definitely comes first," confessed Michels.

"You have to do that," whispered a raspy voice to my right.

Everyone knew that was the inimitable voice of one of the greatest Christians in the history of professional sports.

"Reggie, how you doing?" I inquired.

"Doing good."

"A great victory over the Detroit Lions last week. Tell me about it. I was speaking in a church in Mather and didn't see it," I began. The team had held the Lions to just one touchdown, winning 20-10.

"Looks like the defense must have played particularly well."

Few, especially of late, have been able to enjoy some "White humor" which would be apparent this day as Reggie commented on my observation.

"We shut Barry Sanders down to a mere 105 yards!"

Michels burst out in laughter totally appreciating what his teammate was saying. That is quite a feat against the light-footed slippery Lion.

"So, that's pretty good," laughed a proud White.

"We made him look mortal," chimed John.

I asked White why it seemed that the team didn't quite appear to have the same fire as the year before. (A bit later I used the word

Reggie makes a point as he looks at Steve during the show.
John and Reverend Kevin Penniman listen in.

complacency. He didn't totally agree, but didn't dismiss it either.)

"We still are hungry, like last year, but it's been a long year for us with two minicamps, then with regular camp July 11th, and then with five pre-season games. So, in many respects, we were both mentally and physically tired," he admitted candidly.

So often the fans complain about the record. Reggie shed some powerful honesty with regard to what he shared with his teammates just days earlier when some complaining hit the locker room.

"We were five and two; some of the guys said we should be seven-and-oh. I told them we could just as easily have been oh-and-seven. Mike gave us a break (over the bye week) and I think that helped us a lot."

I asked him if it was tough to play against the Eagles, his former team. We had lost to them in the second game of the year.

"It's not really too tough 'cause if you start beating those guys those people will boo them out of the stadium," he said as we chuckled. "We just didn't do the things that we needed to do."

After a break, I challenged Reggie with the same thought I had brought up a year earlier on the show. Why is it so important to win?

"People don't have a whole lot of respect for losers. My son, about four years ago, even though I was playing for the Green Bay Packers, was a fan of the Dallas Cowboys and the San Francisco 49ers."

"Wow," I laughed surprisingly.

"That's because they were winning."

"Has he been delivered from that?" I interrupted.

"He hasn't been delivered from the "Cowboy thing," but we're prayin' for him," he chuckled as everyone in the studio "lost it." Now came the classic Reggie preaching we knew to expect.

"People underestimate winning. What Jesus did on the cross and what He did for us, He did with a winning attitude. The Bible says, 'Thanks be to God that we have victory in Jesus Christ our Lord,' so His whole mission was to win."

White went further. "I agree with Vince Lombardi that winning is everything; we have an enemy in the devil who we don't want to lose to. So, we have to have the attitude of winning against him. We know we already have that victory through Jesus."

"John and I have talked many times about the fact that people think we as Christians are wimps. What they don't know is Jesus wasn't a wimp. If Jesus played left tackle for the Packers, he would "pancake" the guy (flatten him to the turf). Then he'd help him up, look him in the eye and say, 'I can't let you get to my quarterback.'" I asked my co-host why he thought Christians settle for this misconception, which he addressed with his usual insight.

"Jesus stepped on peoples' toes. Jesus was bold and He got into peoples' lives. And His message was, 'I may tear father and son apart. I may tear mother and daughter apart because you know what? You can't let anything stand in the way of my relationship with you.' He was bold and aggressive and turned the tables over in the temple," said a fired up Michels about his Savior.

"That's what He calls us to be. The same thing with the game we play. Of course, He doesn't want us to be dirty and go outside of the rules, but He wants us to do everything as unto Him and to be champions just as Reggie said because that's the way we can preach the message."

Speaking of bold, here comes another nugget of truthful boldness from ol' number 92.

"You mention about the wimp part," said White looking at me with his arms crossed. "I listened to Ted Turner one time when he said Christians are wimps and I was really angry with him. But you know what? After a while I thought about it and I agree with Ted. Most Christians are wimps!"

"I told a friend of mine," he admitted, "that I should write a book called, Punks, Wimps and Wannabes."

Again we laughed, but underneath it was some conviction for all of us in that studio.

"It's almost like Christians tell the devil, 'Stay over there and leave me alone, and I promise I won't do anything.' We don't want any hard times, we don't want any suffering. And the Bible says Jesus learned his obedience through suffering. We don't want the hard part of what it takes to be a Christian and we do everything to stay out of the hard times and out of Satan's way."

Reggie's really fun when the mics are off, according to Steve.
White shares with the guys during a break.

He continued on his roll. "But men of God like Jesus taught us that Jesus went up in the Pharisees' faces and called 'em a bunch of vipers and hypocrites. They couldn't touch Him until it was time to be touched. He wasn't a punk or chump walking around with a sad face like they show on TV. This man was a man of authority and that's why people followed Him."

I asked White to talk about how he found himself in Green Bay, even amidst some confusion on his part. He seemed grateful that I had asked.

"Well, it's amazing you just asked that question because God showed me something after the Minnesota game last year," he acknowledged. "The Lord spoke to me and said, 'Reggie, why do you think I wanna give you an opportunity to win a championship.' And I said I know it's not cause of my faith. And the Lord spoke to me and confirmed that saying, 'Because your definition of faith is wrong.'"

He went on to point out that God said to him that faith is not so much the expectation that something was going to happen or the "name it and claim it," but as it says in Hebrews 11 that it's more about doing what

God wants us to do in obedience. This was just another great teaching from the man many know as a football player. Listeners were being blessed by the man of God.

Boy, are we ever glad this man had been obedient in 1993 when he arrived in Titletown USA. He looked at me again and confirmed, "As you said, everybody including myself, thought I was crazy when I came to Green Bay." Reggie, we don't think so anymore.

Michels couldn't resist coming in with some great commentary on the matter before our next break. "The word faith is definitely one of the most misinterpreted words out there. When people hear that word they say, 'Faith, yeah, I have faith. I believe in God.' Well, Satan believes in God and Satan knows God exists and knows what God can do."

"And the demons tremble," I added.

Reggie chimed in with perfect harmony, "And they obey His voice. When He tells them to do something, they do it!"

"The Bible is filled with examples of it. They were pleading with Him to go in the swine," added Michels.

White acknowledged the fact that it is pastors who should be the leaders in the world, but the fact of the matter is, right or wrong, the athletes like him have been given the platform.

"When we walk into communities, and I've been down to Milwaukee and I've been to inner cities, people know who we are. People will listen to us because of what we do. They want to touch us and see what we're about. There are many of us who are mature enough to be able to take on that responsibility and be the leaders."

"The problem becomes one of territorial issues when it comes to churches, pastors and other Christians. They don't really want to push guys out there to have that kind of influence."

Those were pretty strong words. Right or wrong, you can't deny their influence as Green Bay Packers. After all, you are reading this book, aren't you?

To add to the point, John talked about how he met Reggie while in high school. "I was one of six hundred kids in an auditorium only because Reggie White was there and he shared the Gospel. I can't tell you what an impact that had on my life." Amen.

We took a break. I've learned that when the mics are off, that's when a sweetness and candidness can be felt in both words and body language, which simply is not possible in other settings. For example, Reggie launched into this harangue about why Christ was crucified. It was so profound I made sure he would share it later. It's worth the price of this book.

Upon returning from the commercials, things really lightened up. For a while it got downright silly. As you may or may not know, White is a huge professional wrestling fan. I wouldn't have been much of a talk-show host if I hadn't asked him to comment on the match he had during the off-season with former Packer Steve McMichael. Incidentally, Reggie lost.

"Reg, I want you to know, I took your loss hard, but I haven't lost any respect for you."

Before I could even finish, Reggie was roaring. Friends, just once I wish you could hear him laugh, either on or off radio, on or off television. This man loves to have fun. It's a shame the media doesn't show you this side of him very often. Reggie took time to explain what many in our audience were now wondering about.

"It was funny because I got attacked by the Christian community suggesting that I shouldn't be doing stuff like that. But I tell people, I say 'Look, I'm not going to live a boring life like you do.'" Again, we all laughed at the big fella who was eating up this chance to explain himself, but not before Michels came out with some tongue-in-cheek wisdom.

Looking at White he said, "I'm not gonna be a punk, wimp or wannabe!" I took the insanity one step further. I reminded Reggie that McMichael had hit Reggie in the back with a brief case before pinning our hero. (Apparently, someone had taken Reggie's mind off of the match for just a moment.)

"We got a young kid in the Packer locker room who does equipment and he told me, 'Reggie, don't you ever let a woman get your attention like that again!'" This time Reggie was laughing at himself with a deep, earth-shaking belly laugh. I'm not sure if many people even have a clue about this multimillionaire man of God who has the capacity for such humor!

"Reggie, give us the scoop," I asked. "Will there be a rematch?"

"Probably not."

I was about to introduce Kevin Penniman to the crew. I pointed out to White, "Reggie, this may come as a big surprise to you, but we don't have many African American people in Green Bay, like they do in Rockford, Illinois."

White laughed once again, knowing what I was trying to say. "They just play for the Packers," he joked, imitating what many people have said. I asked Kevin if the Packers were having a positive influence even in Illinois.

"When people hear of someone like Reggie White and John Michels in a world where we have so many bad, and I mean bad, role models, it does a lot of good. I see teenagers all the time who don't wanna rock the boat." And then Penniman came out with some of the finest wisdom that's ever hit the airwaves.

"God calls us to be more than conquerors; we just don't want to have anything to have to conquer. But when you see people like these guys who don't care what the media says and who pray on the 50-yard line, it challenges our youth and all Christians to be bold in the Lord," he said. "That attitude is contagious."

It was time for the "classic of all classic" Reggie as he shared some insight as to why Jesus Christ was so despised by so many while He walked the earth 2000 years ago. I asked him to share what he had been talking with us about during the break.

"Back there during Jesus' day, one of the reasons He was crucified was because He affected the local economy. He was healing people, so it affected the medical field. He was raising people from the dead, so it affected the funeral homes and graveyard business."

We couldn't hold it in any longer. As true as it no doubt was, it was all so bizarrely profound that we just had to laugh... It felt good, but White was not through.

"He was feeding people, so it was taking people away from the restaurant business. And then I tell people the worse thing He did that I really believe got Him crucified was that He went in and cleaned out the church."

"That's right," said Rev Kev.

"Oh, yeah," John, Bob and I sighed collectively as if a light had come on. All of a sudden it became really quiet in the studio.

"After He did that they said, 'We got to kill this joker!' Bring that into today," Reggie challenged. "If everybody started getting saved, it would effect the economy of this whole country. If everybody started doing what is right, there would be no illicit sex. There would be no pornographic material. There would be no smoking. There would be no more drugs. We'd clean this country up."

"As I said earlier," he reiterated, "that's why I think many Christians are wimps. It's because we don't want the powerful to come against us. We don't want to go where Satan really is in his domain and say, 'We're going to kick your tail.' We just want to play with the little demons. Until Christians start shaking up the world around them, we're not going to see a difference in this country." It was a rap.

We snapped a few pictures and then we split. Is it any wonder that this man was chosen by God to profess the Gospel? On this day, as usual, Reggie blessed me. I'm sure as you've digested these pages, I'm probably not alone.

If you would like a tape of this or any other
"Leap of Faith Sports Radio Show", call us at (800) 236-1549.
We would be happy to send you an order blank.

CHAPTER 16

Rawhide
Once More

One of the truly great stories which epitomizes the influence the Green Bay Packers have had on the state of Wisconsin is the Rawhide episode. With apologies to those who have heard this precious tale, it involved the marriage of the dreams of John Gillespie and Bart Starr. Over dinner thirty-three years ago, a wonderful youth rehabilitation program was born.

Through the efforts of the Gillespies, Starrs, numerous Packer players and even Vince Lombardi, Rawhide has become one of the most successful programs in the nation. Youth professionals from other countries, including Russia, come to the boys ranch in rural New London, Wisconsin, to study how they achieve a remarkable 80% success rate with juvenile boys. But it was not always so.

There were difficult times, especially in the beginning. One time in particular, Rawhide had its fire nearly doused. As some may recall from Leap 1, it was then that Lombardi allowed Starr to "pitch" the plans for the project to the players in the locker room. Twenty-thousand dollars later, the Rawhide Boys Ranch was on its way.

In Leap 2 we revealed that thanks to the benevolence of Bill and Eddie Woods the ranch gained a $500,000 piece of property which the ranch uses to teach the guys about the outdoors. A $200,000 trust fund was established by the Woods to maintain the property.

Recently I had the joy of running into Bart Starr.

"Bart, do you think John (Gillespie) has one more Rawhide story he can share for Leap 3?" I quizzed. Just as Bart had with the Packers in the huddle, he made the right call.

"If there is somebody who has one, it's John," he said. He was right.

Within a couple of days I was on the phone with Gillespie and God has seen to it that we release the details here of one more great episode with a happy ending.

It's the story of a young man who came to Rawhide courtesy of a

Roger Davenport with his hero Bart Starr.

Washington County Juvenile Judge. His situation, like all the others, was dealt with delicately and lovingly, yet with non-compromising Christian principles. Meet Roger Davenport. To say Roger was heading down the wrong path would be as accurate as Michael Jordan is when only ten feet away from the bucket. While his first few months were difficult, God saw to it that this young man's brokenness would open the door to his heart and help him become the man he is today.

The setting is the early eighties. Davenport found himself in the care of loving houseparents Rich and Janet King. Roger convinced the staff he did not want to be at Rawhide. They had decided to send him back to his county juvenile court. John and Jan Gillespie's son, Tim, was a teenager the same age as Roger and had developed a good relationship with Davenport.

Tim went to the Kings and asked them a question that made a world of difference in the life of Roger Davenport. "Is it possible to have Roger come and stay with us?"

After prayerful consideration, they agreed. "If it will help Roger, sure."

With the Gillespies' efforts, and a great deal of dedication, commitment and hard work on Roger's part, things began to fall into place. We've heard the phrase, "If it is to be, it's up to me." Truer words were never spoken, and they were especially pertinent in Roger's case. With gentle nudges of encouragement from the Starrs, as well, Davenport developed healthy expectations of himself. His esteem rose to a new level. He matured and left Rawhide a changed man.

Roger studied diligently and obtained his real estate license. He and his family bought a wholesale food distribution business. He worked tirelessly calling on stores and restaurants around the Midwest. The business grew and was profitable.

Everyone knows that behind every good man there is an even better woman. In 1984 God blessed Roger with a bride named Sue, a great Christian girl. She has been a tireless business partner, a great mother and strong spiritual encouragement to Roger.

After selling the food company, Roger took his share of the profits and purchased a runned-down 1,100-acre game preserve in northern Wisconsin, Three Lakes Preserve in Three Lakes. With over 500 head of

Roger Davenport with his lovely wife Sue and their children,
Sean, Sydney and Abe.

white-tailed deer and nearly 100 trophy bucks, it has become one of the most popular hunting destinations in the country. People fly in from all across America to spend a week or weekend at the beautiful lodge sitting on the bluff overlooking Davenport's private lake.

How was this success story made possible? It was through the love, encouragement and role modeling of Bart and Cherry Starr and the Gillespie family. The connection Davenport feels for the Starrs continues today. Roger recently made the three-hour trek to Appleton to spend a day with his mentors.

In a chartered plane, Roger joined both John and Bart for a flight to a state convention where Starr spoke on behalf of Rawhide. It meant a great deal to Roger. "This is one of the most special days of my life-- spending it with Bart Starr."

Another special day occurred last fall when Roger and his former housefather, Rich King, sat quietly in a deer blind in the center of Roger's preserve. In the chill of the morning just after daylight, Rich looked at Roger with tears in his eyes. "Roger, sitting here with you today as brothers in Christ is precious. Your life is a testimony of God's blessing upon our efforts at Rawhide."

I'm sure the Kings struggled years earlier with the decision to release Roger to the care of others. However, they knew that there are times when, if you truly love someone, you must let him go and pray he returns. Roger did.

The legend of the Rawhide Boys Ranch lives on. Current Packers, like Reggie and Sara White, and Adam and Jan Timmerman, have been to Rawhide to meet the 70 boys and to share their testimonies. For the past three decades the Christian role-modeling exhibited by Bart and Cherry Starr has provided a rock-solid value system for the boys.

Thanks to their courage to follow through on this vision, dozens of other servants of God, whose lives have been changed, remain strong and faithful today because of the ranch. And many continue to experience the love of God through dedicated Christian staff every day at the boys ranch.

An 80% success rate? That's phenomenal in any recovery program. What's the secret? According to Gillespie, "It's 2,000 years old. It is finding quality staff who live the values of Jesus Christ before the boys; it's not to preach to them, but to embrace every one of them with the same tough but unconditional love which the Lord extends to each and every one of us"...the same love that's only a Rawhide leap of faith away.

CHAPTER 17

The Packer Hall of Faith

• THE WHITE WALL •

The Packer Hall of Faith
• THE WHITE WALL •

Bryce Paup

Born: February 29, 1968
Died:

Green Bay Packers   1990-1994
(currently with JAX)
#95   Linebacker
UNI
Drafted by GB in 6th rd
HT: 6-4   WT: 265

An ordained minister, Paup will serve at his home church, Bayside Christian Fellowship, after his career in the NFL is over.   Enjoys snowmobiling, golf, lifting weights, fishing and working on old cars.

Inducted into the Packer Hall of Faith as a player in 1998

Steve Rose and Bryce Paup at a 1998 fund-raiser for Wisconsin Congressional candidate Chuck Dettman.

I'm sure the folks back in Scranton, Iowa, home of the Trojans, knew Bryce Paup would be a great NFL football player and even would make it to the Pro-Bowl someday. Yeah, sure...and blizzards from the Dairy Queen are calorie free. It didn't surprise God, however, who had "the plan" in action since Paup was only four years old.

It was one of the great days in my life when I met Bryce Paup in January of 1995. It is so vividly recorded in my memory because that's the day Ken Ruettgers introduced me to Ben and Jerry's ice cream. It seemed like the biggest deal of the day until I met Bryce.

Bryce Paup went from being an average All-Pro with the Packers that season to an all-out superstar in the NFL by the following year. Unfortunately he did it while with the Buffalo Bills after the Packers let him go.

Paup, like many of his cohorts, exuded class and humility when I met him. For a superstar, he is one of the most down-to-earth players I have ever had an opportunity to know.

The greatest story about Bryce has nothing to do with football. Thanks to rearing by Byron and Harriet Paup, one the finest men of God has had the chance to increase Gods' kingdom with his actions, words and a book. His testimony of finding Christ as Savior is one of the cutest you'll ever hear. I asked him during the radio show in '95 about it.

"Bryce, when did you come to know the Lord?"

"At the age of four," he said without hesitation.

"Why did you wait so long?"

"I had struggled so long," he said through Ken's and my chuckling.

"That was my first experience and a lot of people say, 'You don't know what you are doing when you are four years old,' but I knew exactly what I was doing. There was an altar call given (a chance to accept Christ) and I knew I had to be up there.

Paup shared that giving your all to the Lord can be tough, but especially as a pro athlete he needed God more than ever. He reiterated this in his book, <u>What's Important Now</u> (Multnomah Books), released this past off-season.

This last June, I had the chance to do a fundraiser for a friend and saw Bryce there. He looked great (three-percent body fat!) and was as kind and as gracious as ever. My heart still breaks remembering how God moved Paup on to Buffalo from the Packers in 1995. He is now in Jacksonville where he will, hopefully, finish out his football career. Then, he'll begin a new "career" in ministry with his mentor, Arni Jacobson, at Bayside Christian Fellowship in Green Bay, Bryce's home church.

Without any more words, we present the boy from Scranton, Iowa, into the Green Bay Packer Hall of Faith.

The Packer Hall of Faith
• THE WHITE WALL •

Eugene Robinson

Born: May 28, 1963
Died:

Green Bay Packers   1996-1997
#41   Free safety
Colgate
Acquired in trade in 1996
HT: 6-0   WT: 197

Worked with the MDA in Washington. Did benefits for the Boys and Girls Clubs in Seattle. Has also worked with the Union Gospel Mission. Had his own TV show in Green Bay. Earned a B.S. degree in computer science. Plays the saxophone.

Inducted into the Packer Hall of Faith as a player in 1998

Eugene Robinson is the most exuberant "light" that has ever passed through Green Bay. If you are looking for the best combination of a star, who has a great attitude and is a man of God, he's your man. What you saw with Eugene was what you got. He gleamed like a torch with the Spirit of the Lord as his fuel.

I met Eugene on that fabulous day in 1997 when we recorded "The Gang" in the "LOFSRS" studios. I fell in love with him then, and that love increased every time I saw him. A man of a million words, he was and continues to be upbeat. Hearts are still broken with the thought of Robinson finishing his career in Atlanta. He arrived here when the Packers parted with Matt LaBounty to the Seahawks.

Eugene was a great role model and man of God while he was here. He never withheld something if it was important to him and has been quite candid as to why he has done what he has done since 1985 in the NFL. He shared this during his two times on the show.

"I want to leave a legacy to my kids of following Jesus Christ," he professed. "And, I want to use my platform to reach people for Christ, that's all. When I'm speaking to the media, it's for them, not anyone else," he would say.

There was only one other guy I'd met in my time doing the radio show that was as much a magnet of hope and love with a light that filled the room. That was Keith Jackson. Both were bent on seeing people come to Jesus Christ and also on sharing with others how they could take that current relationship to the next level.

I still feel the hug Gene gave me after one of his TV shows at the Paper Valley in Appleton. Of all the Packer pictures which adorn my wall at home, I smile most when I see the one of us.

Friends, and those of you who have grown to love him, be assured of this. The reason he left Green Bay was not about playing second string, money or anything else. It was about one thing. God wanted him in Atlanta.

There is, however, one place where Robinson will remain forever in addition to the millions of hearts in Packerland. That's the Packer Hall of Faith where we induct him right now. God bless Eugene Robinson, a man who did so much here in such a little time and all of it to advance the kingdom of Jesus Christ.

The Packer Hall of Faith
• THE WHITE WALL •

Ken Ruettgers

Born: August 20, 1962
Died:

Green Bay Packers   1985-1996
#75   Offensive tackle
USC   Drafted by GB first rd
HT: 6-6   WT: 295

Hosted an annual Girls and Boys Club tournament in
Bakersfield each year. Involved in the Children's Miracle
Network, Diabetes Foundation, and the 65 Roses Club which
helps raise funds for Cystic Fibrosis. Easter Seals and Special
Olympics have also benefited over the years from Ken's time.
Politics and gold keep him busy. Holds a B.S. degree in busi-
ness administration and an M.B.A. degree from Cal-State
Bakersfield. Wrote a bestselling book, <u>Home Field Advantage</u>,
released in 1995.

Inducted into the Packer Hall of Faith in 1998

What can I say about Ken Ruettgers? Plenty! What I most want to acknowledge is that his character and integrity are above reproach. His love for his family transcends anything he ever did as a football player for the Green Bay Packers.

My mind journeys back to a "freeze frame." Jim Irwin, the longtime voice of the Packers, announced the Packers' first-round pick in 1985. I was turning left onto Commercial Street from Congress in Neenah. "Who is Ken Ruettgers?" I thought. Ten years later, I'd find out.

The media had me absolutely convinced by the time I met him in 1994 that he was the biggest jerk in the world. He had held out, as Ken would later tell me, to "maximize his opportunity" three times while in a Packer uniform. Each time the team met his demands and he followed through with great performances. He had a poor relationship with the media and he loved Rush Limbaugh.

Despite what I had heard, I met the neatest person in that WORQ radio studio on September 27, 1994. My life has never been the same since. I treasure the day God put him into my life. It has led to this, the third book in the "Leap" trilogy, and the network radio and TV shows. Don't expect him to take the credit cause he'll give it to Jesus.

Truth is, there isn't anything left for me to say that I haven't said already, so I will spare you, move on, and not embarrass my friend any longer. Without further delay, I present Ken Ruettgers as member #001, the first to be enshrined into the Green Bay Packer Hall of Faith. Thanks, partner. I love you. You're the greatest.

The Packer Hall of Faith
• THE WHITE WALL •

Bart Starr

Born: January 9, 1934
Died:

Green Bay Packers
1956-1971   1975-1983
#15 Quarterback/Head coach
Alabama   Drafted by GB 17th rd in 1956
HT: 6-0   WT: 195

Super Bowl I and II MVP. Co-founder of the Rawhide
Boys Ranch. Fund raiser for numerous charities. Helped
the Jaycees of Wisconsin. Too many other achievements
and accomplishments to list here.

Inducted into the Packer Hall of Fame in 1977

Inducted into the Packer Hall of Faith as player and coach
in 1998

A name says so much, and "Starr" says it all about Bart's time in Green Bay. So admirable and affable, from the moment he arrived in Green Bay, he became a favorite. It was not because of the plays that he made or the work that he did, but because of the person that he is.

It has been documented in each of the books of this series that Bart and Cherry Starr co-founded the Rawhide Boys Ranch with John and Jan Gillespie in 1965. His heart and passion for God, for his teammates and for the community was so omnipresent.

In fifth grade I read a book about how Bart would take all the kids in the community out for burgers at McDonalds after playing football in his backyard, and that he was one of the most pleasant, moral folks you could ever spend time with.

As we researched for these books, a great story about Starr surfaced. It was this. Few know that he gave away both of the Corvettes that he won for being MVP in each of the first two Super Bowls. He is a man whose thoughts and actions have always been focused to help make the world a better place.

Our minds fill with reminiscings of his quarterback sneak to beat the Dallas Cowboys on that dreadfully cold day at Lambeau. We remember how, with class and honor, he led this team in the GM and head coach capacity. When I learned that he was released of these duties in 1983, I felt awful, as if the family dog had been taken out in the woods and shot. It was painful. Bart, however, took it all with class.

Bart Starr is not "eligible" for heaven because of all he has done, or because of his honesty and morals. Oh, no. Like everyone else, his requirement is the same. He asked Christ to forgive him of his sins, past and present, and has accepted Jesus Christ as his Lord and Savior. He did that years ago and today does a good job of putting feet to that faith.

The Packer Hall of Faith is not a place where Starr sneaked in like during the '66 season championship. His place has been reserved forever. Mr. Starr, welcome. Your impact has been beyond imagination around "Titletown."

The Packer Hall of Faith
• THE WHITE WALL •

Adam Timmerman

Born: August 14, 1971
Died:

Green Bay Packers   1995-
#63   Offensive guard
South Dakota State
Drafted by GB in 7th rd
HT: 6-4   WT: 295

He and wife, Jan, are honorary chairpersons for the March of Dimes. Has been involved in various fundraisers in the off-season. Has his own radio show. Speaks at various churches and schools.   Holds a B.S. degree in agriculture business. Hobbies include fixing up old cars and farming.

Inducted into the Packer Hall of Faith as a player in 1998

It was August 13, 1995, and the Packers were playing a pre-season game. Only Packer fans care about pre-season games. The nationally-televised game was against the Pittsburgh Steelers; it was one of the hottest days of the summer. The cameras flashed to the sidelines and a young red-headed man sporting a 60's style flat-top haircut. He had a grin from ear to ear and really looked like he was enjoying himself. His number was 63.

The following Monday I learned his name was Adam Timmerman. I was sure he would be one of the training camp casualties. After all, what are the chances of a guy from South Dakota State making it with the Packers anyway? Well, God wasn't thinking the way I was; I sure am glad.

On September 4, 1995, I met this special "bulldog" who was still wearing that grin. As he walked down the hall to the radio studio, Ken intercepted him and introduced him to me. To watch where God has taken this very regular kind of guy over these years is quite amazing.

I keep talking about our Lord who, more than ability, honors availability, Adam is another example of this. His commitment to Christ really exploded as he has been woven in with the other believers on the Packers. The spiritual growth that those around him have seen is impressive. He regularly has Jan on his arm as he shares what his personal relationship with Jesus Christ has done for his life.

Like Paup, (it must be those Iowa roots), he is another of the most down to earth Packer players I have met. We always tease one another when we're together. I have to say he has the best sense of humor (with some consideration to Pepper Burruss).

Our laughs together turned to tears for me as I listened to a "sentence sermon" that Adam gave me on May 29, 1998. Timmerman and I were at a benefit together in Madison. My father, David Rose, was with me. It was my dad's 71st birthday. The lineman had lost his father, 51, in an ATV accident earlier that month back home on the family farm in Cherokee, Iowa.

As we walked off the platform on which we had both been, he had a few, select words for me that thunder through my mind still.

Timmerman put his right arm around my father's shoulder and looked me directly in the eyes.

"Don't take this guy for granted."

No more words were needed. I got the message. In a selfish way, if it was to deliver those words that had been the only reason God brought Timmerman to Green Bay, I will be eternally grateful. Needless to say, there is more. Another reason was to secure his place once and for all in the Packer Hall of Faith. With a grin, I'm sure, here comes the South Dakota Jackrabbit and the newest member here, Adam Timmerman.

Adam Timmerman speaks at a WIPSAC benefit in Madison.

The Packer Hall of Faith
• THE WHITE WALL •

Reggie White

Born: December 19, 1961
Died:

Green Bay Packers   1993-
#92   Defensive end
Tennessee
Acquired as free agent in 1993
HT: 6-5   WT: 304

Received a B.A. degree in human services. Has been involved in a plethora of charities and causes that are too numerous to identify here. Loves professional wrestling; took the ring in 1997 against former Chicago Bear and Packer teammate Steve McMichael.

Inducted into the Packer Hall of Faith as a player in 1998

Green Bay never has and never will be the same since Reggie White arrived. If anybody had any doubts about who he serves, those should have been eliminated by now. His Leader and Master is his Lord and Savior, Jesus Christ. Everything he does is with an end in mind. That end is to help others find out what is so amazing about God's saving grace.

Reggie Howard White is, without question, the man who took the Packers to a whole new level spiritually. There is something very real, proper, but yet just like the mystery of God, that he is the last man to be inducted here in this book. Scripture talks many times about the last being first and the first being last. I think that is very apropos here, as well.

To waste this space talking about football would be a betrayal to the kingdom of heaven. After all, Lambeau Field, as of late, has just been the ground from which Reggie has bounded to take the Body of Christ to a whole new plateau.

This gutsy man's achievements, sacks, tackles and other statistics will eventually wind up in the Pro Football Hall of Fame and the Green Bay Packer one, no doubt. Like the rest of the gold trophies and Super Bowl rings, they will burn someday. They are no big deal to White.

I think of the man who died and stood before the Lord at the gate of heaven holding bricks of gold. "Oh, look," said Jesus, "pavement!"

Reggie White obediently and faithfully came to Green Bay to tell you one thing. It's this. Without a personal profession of your faith in Jesus Christ to forgive your sins, you can't get to heaven. It's that simple, plain and clear. You can't be good enough on your own...not because Reggie White says so, but because God says so. (Ephesians 2:8-9)

In the course of my travels, I have been asked how one could meet Reggie White or get a message to him and I am left empty-handed for answers. As I've mentioned for years, if there were 92 of Reggie, there still wouldn't be enough of him to go around. However, I don't need much of a leap of faith to make you one guarantee right now. It is this. You can meet Reggie White someday!

If you will bow your heart before God and accept Christ as Savior, you are sure to see Reggie in heaven. With him will be a few others you will also recognize. You'll find they are as normal as you are.

With great pleasure I stand with "the man with the plan," Reggie White. I thank you, bold one, for teaching us to stand firm and not to be concerned with what others think as we profess God's truth. May you enjoy your eternal stay here in the warm confines of the Packer Hall of Faith, the one for

CHAPTER 18

Does God Still Love the Packers?

My bumper stickers "God Must Be A Packer Fan" were regularly disappearing from the back fender of my car. I was having a little trouble figuring out if the Packer faithful here in Wisconsin just wanted to have one for their own car or.... Or had God himself become so ashamed of the team after the Super Bowl loss, He'd sent out legions to rip them off my vehicle?

Honestly, I never got an answer on that one, but God has left us clues in His Word as to His faithfulness. He loves us no matter what. I guess it was only fair that people were, both then and still today, asking me the question. "Steve, what's the deal? If God is a Packer fan, why did we lose the Super Bowl?" A great question with a logical response.

I hope to give you answers that will be appropriate, not just for today or tomorrow, but forever. If you carefully read the two previous books in this trilogy, they will confirm that we never said God has ever caused the Packers to win. Never. What the books have boldly proclaimed by the Spirit of God is this. Where God is given honor, He will respond. For example, when men or women of God stand and profess the gospel of Jesus Christ, He uses them.

Are we saying that because Reggie White, Robert Brooks, or Christians from the team's past have told people about the saving grace of Christ, He's chosen this team to speak to the world? Is this why God has brought the team to the forefront in the sports world? The Leap of Faith series was spurred by the haunting reality that the mainstream media wouldn't touch the "miracles" which began with Reggie's elbow in 1994 and continued with his hamstring healing in 1995, not to mention a miracle for which Brett acknowledges divine intervention, also.

Over the years, people and media have challenged that these incidences are, in reality, merely coincidences, or that they can logically be explained. Tell that to Reggie, who has experienced numerous medical phenomena since his arrival in Green Bay in 1993; or to Brett Favre whose ankle injury in 1995 was so serious it took God to repair it so he could play against the Bears. He tried to tell the people via the media. Should we be surprised that information didn't make it to the masses?

What's the key word in all of this? Is it faith? Isn't it ever a Godincidence that not only the godly guys on this team, but others in the world in general who profess Christ as their Savior and Healer, are the ones who experience miracles? Pretty crazy, isn't it? But it's true. The ones who are taking the leap of faith to believe are also the ones experiencing miracles.

Furthermore, because of a personal relationship with Christ, like Reggie, for example, God reveals His heart and intentions to them...the same Spirit who spoke to Reggie in the post 1997 off-season about the fact that he had a commitment and could not yet retire. It's also the same Spirit who told Robert Brooks he was not going to finish the 1996 season! That same Spirit prompted Ken Ruettgers to begin a radio show in 1994, which has ultimately led to these words in front of you.

It's the same Spirit who has told me what to write in this book you're now reading. In some cases, that Spirit specifically told me what to say to individuals when autographing their books.

I don't say these things about myself to impress you, but to impress upon you what can happen when you accept Christ into your heart and life, when you listen to His voice and follow the calling. Like me, you may not be a multimillionaire professional athlete, but God's plan for you is every bit as important as the one for Reggie White!

I believe God has called me to be the "public relations spokesperson" for the Christians in Green Bay, as well as to be the "Packer Evangelist." In a nutshell, He asked me to tell you He chose this team because of the faithfulness and the availability which many of the Christians have brought to the team. Some pretty neat stories, huh? Could they possibly indicate that God's handprints are all over this team?

When did it all start? Only God knows that. When will it end? Only He knows that, too. What I do know is that it's still happening at the time of this writing (June of 1998). It does look, however, like God did take His anointing off the team during the Super Bowl, doesn't it?

I have received assurance from a few of the Super Bowl XXXII players that they did make some mistakes in San Diego. There were both physical as well as spiritual obstacles. It would appear that God allowed a really humbling loss. I'll let the guys explain in more detail throughout this book.

Because we can bring it back onto the field, I need to tell you that the explanations may be mysterious and downright bizarre to you still. Just between the two of us, I contend that it was the Spirit of the Lord who told me the main reason the Packers lost the game.

Two months after the loss I couldn't resist an opportunity which allowed me to expose my true feelings on the subject. God had brought a pastor into my path whose feelings regarding Super Bowl XXXII were congruent with mine. Her words nearly knocked me over. Her name? Pastor Kathryn Kershaw from Oshkosh, Wisconsin.

She approached me after a speaking event in Appleton. Once she had introduced herself, she quickly began to let me know why the Packers had lost the Super Bowl. Curiously I listened. I had predetermined that if the word that came out of her began with a "p" I would faint. It did. (By some power I remained standing!) I suppose I really wasn't that surprised after all.

"Pride is what it was," said the former Texan with a gentle, southern drawl. That is exactly what my spirit had told me right after the game. "God told me this is His team, not the Cowboys or anyone else." Can you imagine how difficult this was for her to admit, especially as a recovering Cowboy fan?

I had to comment. "You know, that's kind of the feeling I had."

She took it a step further. "The Lord told me that He gave them right up until game time to repent and to ask for forgiveness for the pride or any other sins that had been committed that week or day."

Yeah, it's far fetched, but can you perhaps see how "sin in the camp" could disrupt even a team with a strong anointing? A Packerwomaniac (a die hard lady Packer nut) brought everything into perspective. Her letter arrived in my mailbox in February, a month after the Packer loss against Denver. I think a few sentences from it may help bring light to the issue of the spiritual side of the Packers and their fans.

Pam Schlenvogt shared some of her wisdom. "Your books have been very inspirational to me. I have been a Packer fan since I was a little kid, and I love the Lord more than anything. To combine the two is a real Utopia for me!" Pam, you're not alone.

She continued to talk about Leap 1. "The scope of influence the Packers have is enormous. Packer players take this responsibility seriously. What a great love affair, as you put it. Fans must be able to separate their euphoria of the Packers and their love for the Lord. I think some have it turned around." Amen.

I loved what she said about Leap 2. "Because of the Super Bowl loss, fans are at an emotional all time low and I'm glad because now they may be more open to God's Word. Now the healing begins." Yes, if we catch the depths of reality to that statement! John Michels will tell you in a later chapter that I was afraid yet somewhat relieved that the Packers lost the big game. You see, in some respects it is actually easier to reach out and speak with people about spiritual issues at a funeral than at a wedding.

About ten minutes after the Super Bowl XXXII loss, God showed me that fans would be easier to reach with His message from that point until we peaked again. Have you caught it? Friend, in another few pages, the tug from God on your Packer heart could end.

At the close of this book, Pastor Jacobson will give you an opportunity to accept a message that will allow you to realize your very purpose for existence. It with impact both your earthly and eternal life. And if you accept it, I know you'll thank God forever that in His love and mercy He has spoken to you through this team. Yes, God is a Packer fan, but more importantly, He loves you! More confirmation of this truth is just a few more pages and the greatest leap of faith you'll ever take away.

CHAPTER 19

The Leap of Faith Sports Radio Show 97'

Week #13 • "Mr. Robinson"

Show #9713 (Recorded Nov. 17, 1997)
Aired on WSRN stations Nov. 21-23, 1997

Steve Rose and John Michels, co-hosts
Eugene Robinson, guest

I'd fallen asleep for the second half of the game against the Colts. I awoke to hear the announcers saying, "So long!" I had reason to call Bob Gardinier. His wife, Linda, answered.

"Linda, how you doing?"

"Pretty good...under the circumstances," she replied glumly.

"We didn't?" I bolted back, more than a bit shocked.

"Yeah, 41 to 38." I couldn't believe it. I guess I'm glad I nodded off so I didn't have to watch what turned out to be the equivalent of Chinese water torture as the Colts let the clock run down to kick a winning field goal.

Then, I thought of Kim. She and her friend, Cheri, had taken a train to the game in Indianapolis. I had stayed home in order to keep a speaking engagement at a church that night.

The following day I made my way down the steps of the studio to record another precious gift to the radio faithful all over the Midwest. At the bottom of the stairs I saw my partner and Eugene Robinson, each with wrinkles upon their brows. They look perplexed and appeared to be stumped over a crossword puzzle they were working on.

For a split second I was upset. Why weren't these guys sulking and beating their heads against the nearest wall? After all, the day before they had lost to a team who had been oh-and-ten! I made up my mind I was going to demand an answer during the show, not just for myself, but for the fans who would much rather have had toothpicks put down their fingernails than to watch a replay of the game from the day before. I wondered how they could be so calm and unassuming while we Packermaniacs felt the sting of defeat.

Thank the Lord I caught myself before the show started and I came to my senses. This is just a game! Although these guys get paid very well to play a game, that's still all it is.

"Let's go, you guys!" I belted from the studio. Both Michels and the popular Packer safety briskly walked in. Robinson had asked if he could come on the show once more. Just two months prior he had been featured on what will no doubt go down as one of the greatest shows of all time. I was with Brooks, Beebe and both him and John. (Even though they had lost, I thought it would still be okay to have him on, I guess.)

I opened the show with the customary question, "How ya doin'?" to John. With some sort of a sixth sense, Michels turned the tables suspecting that the question may have a more interesting answer if he asked it of me.

"How are you doing today, Steve?"

"I'm doing as good as I can be. A lot better than I would have been about six years ago...had I had the experience that I had yesterday in my living room."

Listen to me. You would have thought that a fire or a tornado had ripped through our place. No, it was a football game! I admit that I suddenly realized I might need some counseling from these brothers. Sensing immediately the ridiculousness of my words, Michels wasted no time with a convicting response. Worse still was the fact that he used some of my own words to do the job.

"It seems like we talk about this every week," he started. "Is it really important in the whole scheme of things whether the Green Bay Packers won on Sunday or not? Unfortunately, yesterday we did not. Hopefully none of our listeners out there are not on the verge of suicide because of it," cracked John.

After listening to all the post-game grumbling from fans, I asked Michels, "Why do we get this feeling that there are explanations which people feel are owed to them?"

Without wasting time, John came to the rescue of the green and gold. "In this league, anybody can beat anybody on any given Sunday. You have to give the Indianapolis Colts a lot of credit for the football game they played last Sunday."

John had done a more than adequate job of defending himself. Number 41 was next.

"Let's bring our guest into the mix. Eugene Robinson is here in his second appearance on the show this year. Eugene, you don't know how good it is to see you today." He decided to have some fun with me.

"Ahhh Iya woooaahooohh waya," he began, as if to portray that he was embarrassed, tongue tied, and unsure as to how to start. "How you doin', Steve?" he laughed. It immediately set a tone of ease in the studio.

"Eugene, John will confirm that we don't sit and dwell on wins and losses during this show." I pointed out what, at the moment, was an apparent irony. "You know, Gene was here after the Philadelphia game, too!" (We had lost that game as well.) I blew it. That wasn't very nice, but nobody bats a thousand in any league. I gave him the opportunity to give his due and he took full responsibility.

"I thought they played well. We didn't help ourselves. We were somewhat sloppy, our technique wasn't as good, and whenever you miss tackles everybody looks bad," he confessed. "Ten years from now no one is gonna remember this game. It's just football." Speaking of "it's just football," we were just about through talking about it for the day...almost. But, I couldn't help it. I had to teasingly threaten them.

"Look, you guys can lose to the Indianapolis Colts, but you can't lose to the Dallas Cowboys." They happened to be next week's opponent. "Eugene, you've been here a couple years. Talk about this Cowboy thing."

"You know, there's going to be a lot of hype about this thing cause they have beat the Packers seven straight times. That's a lot. Now we have them here."

There isn't a finer guest than Eugene Robinson.
He appeared twice in 1997 on the "LOFSRS".

His next comment could have gotten him tarred and feathered in the wrong Packer neighborhood.

"I think the fans will make more out of the game than the football players on this team will." Ouch! Honestly, not what I wanted to hear. I expected the guys to confess that they would stay in practice and prayer all week and give us a guarantee of victory.

"Our goal is not to beat the Dallas Cowboys and win a Super Bowl. That's not going to happen because we are in the same conference. My Super Bowl is not against the Dallas Cowboys. My Super Bowl is against whomever makes it there from the AFC," he said.

John talked about his experience with this rivalry. "I got letters when I got here from people saying I hope you help us beat Dallas. It's amazing how much emphasis is put on one game. Last week on the Jumbotron (scoreboard at Lambeau Field) there was this big hype..."

"The showdown in Titletown," Eugene interjected.

"I have to agree with Gene 100%. This is just one more game." You know, I guess each of us has the right to differ with our friends' opinions and declare them "wrong" every once in a while, right? I warned them one more time that it is not the consensus among the fans. Eugene finally comforted us a bit.

"I don't want to make it sound like it isn't important, it is. But, it's not the whole season. Understand that whoever comes into Lambeau Field, they're gonna get their "cranium cracked" cause we're gonna play some ball! Dallas, you happen to be coming in here, let's strap it on!" he finished strongly.

Then some hard facts came out. Robinson couldn't believe them. John had read in Leap 2, and had heard of some other accounts, of fans who take all this a little...no, a lot, too seriously.

"There are families that split up over this."

I fired in, "Hey, domestic abuse rises in Wisconsin after Packer games."

"Are you serious?" asked an amazed Robinson with raised voice.

"That's an absolute fact," I assured.

Michels chimed, "I've heard that it's true nationally, not just in Wisconsin."

"Are you serious?" Gene asked one more time, hoping to be told this was all some sort of joke.

"Oh no, Gene, I'm not kidding."

"They're taking it too serious!" Hello!! That's why I've written two books and the one you are holding now.

"Super Bowl Sunday," Michels added, "is supposedly the greatest day of domestic abuse in this country," Is there a sadder fact than that?

"They are taking this way too seriously. Football is not that important."

"It's our jobs," said Michels, inferring that if there was anyone who could take it seriously, it could be one of them. After all, most of them have million dollar jobs on the line.

I took this opportunity to publicly acknowledge our appreciation of the Reggie Whites, Don Beebes, Eugene Robinsons and John Michels who spread the word that in a hundred years, or even ten seconds from now, when the Lord returns, that this matter of football will mean nothing. All that will matter is where you stand in God's eyes. Specifically, what have each of us done about Jesus Christ?

John answered the question he had been asked as to why he hadn't been starting. Earlier in the season he lost his job to Ross Verba due to an injury.

"People ask me, 'How can you ride that roller coaster ride. You're a number-one draft pick. You started all those games. You're Super Bowl champs and all of a sudden you are benched going into the playoffs.'"

I loved his retort. "Jesus Christ is the constant in my life and I think," as he laughed, "and I think that's what these people are really lacking. They are riding with the highs of our wins and sinking low enough with our losses that they are going to go out and beat their wives and/or beat their children. You need something in your life that's gonna keep you from riding that roller coaster."

"I'm trying to leave my kids a legacy to know Jesus Christ," said the glib safety. "That's much more important than football. I've said all my career that I'm a Christian that just happens to be a football player. This is my occupation. This is the platform God has given me so I need to maximize on that. That's it. My whole goal in playing professional athletics is to bring people into the kingdom of God." Preach it, brother.

"As far as the media is concerned, let me dove-tail on that. When I talk to media people, it's not for the public. It's for those I'm talking with that God has put in my life at that moment. I'm talking to them about Jesus for them," he confessed.

If it goes anywhere, it's the cherry on the sundae according to Robinson. "If it goes across the airwaves, well, that's just an extra bonus. If they print it, that's a bonus, too. I pray that God would minister to them, not anybody else. If I'm talking to them, I believe the Word of God does not return void."

When we returned from break, I had to "spill the beans" on Gene.

"There is a man in this room who bought a young man a bike." I looked at Eugene with a smile hoping he would take the bait.

"That's my buddy, Miles," he began. "He comes by the house all the time.

Eugene and Steve.

He's one of the kids in the neighborhood who doesn't have a bike. He's five years old and he's always coming into my garage asking, 'Can I ride Brandon's bike? Can I ride Brandon's bike?'" Brandon is Eugene's and his wife, Gia's, son. They also have a daughter, Brittany.

"So, I let him ride it. But, he's like the only kid that does not have a bike in the whole neighborhood. So one day I told him, 'Hey, Miles, I tell you what, man, I'm gonna surprise you.'"

"I went to Fleet Farm and got a bike. I wanted it to be new and shiny because, you know, as a kid you open something up and you want it to be new. I don't want some old hand-me-down. I wanted him to be able to open it and say, 'This is my deal.'" The way it sounded, there was a blessing in it for more than just Miles.

"My son and daughter were just as excited because we try to teach them to be givers. They had the bike and they were bringing it to his house and he wasn't home. But then his mom pulled up and motioned for him to get out of the car. And my daughter and son were like, 'This is yours!' His face lit up and what not, so, that was an easy thing to do because there was a need. That's a big deal for a little boy." And it's also a big deal to hear of such a generous man!

Little Miles doesn't stop in just the Robinson's garage these days. Eugene reported that he's treated like another son and comes in the house and says, "Can I have something to drink? Can I have something to drink?" We laughed as he said he told the little man, "Yeah, baby, the refrigerator is right there!"

I asked John how he was using his testimony to talk about his faith. "I try to give glory to God at least once in every interview that I do. The verse that I sign with my autograph, and we talk about it all the time, is Romans 8:28 that..."we know," as he looked at Eugene across the table and smiled. "I have to use that because this was part of Gene's Bible class he taught today. It's that God will work everything for good for those who love the Lord and are called according to His purposes," finished the big left tackle.

Then he took a shot at the press. "Many times the press will come to you and they'll try to get you to curse the coach and say that you've been wronged. I'm not about to do that because that's not what God wants from me." Michels acknowledged that he was going through a rough time as a Packer and he knows all will work out well.

"God is allowing me to go through these things for a reason. And He's going to use these things that I am going through for His glory. I think that throws the media off because they feel that I should be angry. And I come right out and tell them my faith is why I'm not."

Robinson was asked what he feels people appreciate about him and other Christians like him. "People watch what you do instead of just listening to what you say; and they really want you to be real," he professed.

"As John can tell you from the Bible studies that we do, I try to keep it real. I'm not into 'let's fake it' or 'let me make it seem like I'm better than anybody else.' I'm just as fallible as the next guy. The only difference is that Jesus Christ has saved my life and that now I submit myself to Him. That is the constant battle of the spirit and the flesh which goes on. It's where the rubber of Christianity meets the road."

The sting of truth in the next thought Robinson shared was enough to make any believer cringe. "And, if you're really honest with yourself, you'll realize that you don't love God as much as you think you do! It's demonstrated everyday by what you say and do." Robinson's ex-coach at Seattle, Chuck Knox, used to say, "What you do speaks so loud, no need to hear what you have to say."

We came up to our last break. Eugene needed to make a run for his TV show in Appleton. John and I finished up the show. We snapped a couple quick pictures of Gene and me. As he flew out the door, I couldn't resist the impulse to tell him one more time, "Eugene, remember, you can lose to the Colts, but you can't lose to the Cowboys!" He just smiled.

After the following week, we knew he must have been listening, too.

If you would like a tape of this or any other "Leap of Faith Sports Radio Show", call us at (800) 236-1549. We would be happy to send you an order blank.

CHAPTER 20

Ray Nitschke:
Heavenbound on Route 66

I had no sooner walked into my home when the phone rang. My niece, Sandi, had a question for me. "Steve, who was the lady you were hugging on television?"

"Pastor Jacobson's wife," I proclaimed ready to give answer for my actions. Stay with me, I'll explain. I had just returned from an event which I had forgotten had a statewide television audience. It might possibly go down in the eternal annals as the most life-changing event in many lives of Packer fans and others alike.

An hour previously, I'd just witnessed one of the most beautiful church services ever. The Bible says our eyes have not seen nor ear has heard what awaits those who die in Jesus Christ. A Packer legend had gone to his eternal reward.

"Steve are you going to Ray Nitschke's funeral tomorrow?" asked my friend Chuck Dettman over the phone. Chuck is friends with Bayside Christian Fellowship's Senior Pastor, Arni Jacobson, who would conduct the service. Nitschke, possibly the greatest linebacker to ever play the game, had died unexpectedly of a heart attack on March 8, 1998, in Venice, Florida. His memorial service was scheduled for March 14 at 1 p.m. in Green Bay.

"Man, I don't think I wanna get caught in all the people," I whined, never fully understanding the call God has put on my life with regard to matters such as these. I was especially convicted since I had heard Ray's life had been transformed over the last couple years. Deep down inside I knew I needed to be there.

"You really need to be there," Chuck insisted.

"Okay, brother," I agreed after being totally convinced I was going to miss the boat if I didn't.

"Meet me at the Luxury Suites at noon tomorrow. We'll go from there over to the church. See ya," he finished. It was a date.

At approximately 1:45 p.m. on Saturday, I found myself in the foyer of Bayside's huge worship center along with some of the greatest players the NFL has ever known, Willie Davis, Boyd Dowler, Carroll Dale, Mike McCoy and even the "Mad Stork," Ted Hendricks. Also attending was the voice of the Packers, Jim Irwin, and ESPN personality and author Dick Schaap.

Super Bowl I and II MVP Bart Starr was there. John Gillespe, who had contributed to Leap 1 and Leap 2, and Bart founded the Rawhide Boys Ranch in the mid '60s.

Then I spotted Packer president Bob Harlan who has always treated me well and answered my calls during the writing of my books.

There were so many others there, but the congregation had begun singing, a signal that it was time for the service to start. Chuck and I were led down the aisle and ushered to the front row on the far left side of the huge sanctuary. As I unpretentiously gazed around the sanctuary, I spotted Jerry Kramer, Max McGee, Paul Hornung, Ron Wolf and a couple of others.

Old number 66 and his wife Jackie had lovingly adopted three wonderful children, John, Richard and Amy, who were sitting in the front and center next to Ray's picture and the flowers. Like his wife's funeral, there was no casket. Ray had chosen to be cremated so he could be remembered as he was in life, not in death.

The music was rich, pure and reverent as angelic voices sang. It's quite silly, maybe even downright crazy, to have felt this way while sitting at a funeral. I had never heard of a funeral referred to as a celebration, but that's what this one felt like.

After three songs, Pastor Jacobson welcomed the huge congregation of approximately 900 and told us that we would sing three more of Ray's and Jackie's favorite songs. Words from the broad overhead were projected on the wall and the throng of participants made a remarkably joyful noise

The first Leap of Faith book signing in 1996 in Tampa, Florida. Steve Rose is flanked by Ray Nitschke.

joining with the worship team to exalt the Lord Jesus.

And then we sat in silence as the sweet presence of Christ fell over the congregation. Amy Klaas, the Nitschkes' only daughter, accepted the podium. Her words riveted every heart there. She acknowledged being deluged with touching memory after memory all week of her father. It didn't take long to realize she had become overwhelmed by an awareness of just how many lives he had touched. It also became apparent that he meant something different to her than to most of us.

"I didn't know Dad when he played football. I just knew him as my father. All of you sharing your stories of how he touched your life has moved me. I've known him as a giver and as a loving man. I hope all of you remember him for that."

In a strained and broken voice she tried to finish before the grief overcame her. "I praise God for bringing me into his life 26 years ago. He was the best father I could ever have. I will miss him dearly." When she returned to the pew, her husband Jon and brother John each clutched one of her hands as tears poured down her face, her chin to her chest.

Minister of music Rev. Matt Perkins then sang a duet with worship team member Lori Smith. The selection was called, "I Bowed On My Knees and Cried Holy." With the soft but powerful presence of organ accompaniment, Lori began.

With her eyes staring toward heaven and her left hand raised to God, she began, "As I entered the gates I cried holy..." With clenched fist and more emphasis, she continued, "The angels all met me there....." Then

Matt emotionally joined in, "They carried me from mansion to mansion." The worship team joined them to usher the congregation into the presence of Jesus. It was awesome!

John Bankert, NFL Hall of Fame director, approached the platform. "I first met Ray Nitschke about 20 years ago. When I shook his hand, he scared the heck out of me. I last saw him about two months ago. I shook his hand and he still scared the heck out of me. That's just the way he was. His handshake was uncommonly strong, but I don't think he knew it. He had that little mischievous grin on his face and you knew that he liked you."

He went on to explain that Ray took his 1978 induction very seriously, and that if he felt any upcoming inductee wasn't taking it with the honor it deserved, he would let him know about it.

"Glory day" flavor entered the program from those who had known Ray during the greater portion of his life. The first former Packer to eulogize him was former defensive end Willie Davis.

"I can assure you that Ray Nitschke is in this room. He is here in spirit and in character." He told of Ray rebounding from not getting playing time to his All-Pro status. "When I first met Ray Nitschke in 1960, he thought of himself as a judge because he was always sitting on the bench," he said as the crowd softened a bit. "But Ray Nitschke went from the bench to the best middle linebacker on the all time team."

But that wasn't the most impressive thing Willie found about his fellow defensive teammate. "When I first met Ray Nitschke he had every attribute of a sinner. No question in my mind," he said nodding his head from side to side amidst quiet laughter. "But I can tell you that later Ray became a Christian." It was at this moment you could sense the hope permeating the service; perhaps this story was foreordained by the Lord before the beginning of the world. You could also sense a happy ending on the way.

Another man strode up the carpeted stairs. Anyone outside of the Packer glory day circles wouldn't have had a clue who he was.

"My name is Carroll Dale and I'm the "others" listed on the program," he joked as a smattering of laughter erupted. Let me assure you, friend, that on this day he was to be one of the voices of the Lord. He'd be the first to tell you he's a "nobody saved by Somebody" with that "Somebody" being Jesus Christ. And he wasn't afraid to pour out his faith in Jesus, which he had shared with Nitschke over the years. He told his tale of the great Packer linebacker.

"I was Ray's roommate for the last eight years of his career here in Green Bay," he began. He shared a story of a man who wanted to meet Ray while the team was in Chicago to play the Bears. The man tried to sell Ray a toupee. He failed with Ray, but succeeded with Carroll!

He spoke of how Ray would endlessly sign autographs. "We'd tease him saying, 'What are you gonna do, run for office?' but he'd never turn away an autograph seeker. Ray was fantastic."

Then a gleam came to the former Packer receiver as he told of how Ray's wife had shared some great news with him in May of 1996. "Carroll, you would really be proud of Ray. He has found Christ as his personal Savior. He is going to church and worshipping every Sunday. He has found a joy and peace that can only be found in Christ." "It's a big comfort for me to know that," he told the hushed gathering.

Then, what could only have been called a power-packed emotion-laden ten minutes were the memories shared as seen through the eyes of one of Ray's sons, John. He buttoned his suit jacket as he took center stage. "This is great, my father is smiling. I read a lot of nice things about my father this past week. Team player. Warrior. Leader. Winner. Champion. Celebrity. True friend. A man of valor, a man of worth. To Richard, Amy and myself...he was Dad.

"For many people the most important day of their lives, the most pleasant day, is the day they are born. For me, that day came a couple months later when God saw to it that Jackie and Ray Nitschke would be my mother and father. Boy, I'm truly one lucky, blessed person. I guess the greatest thing a son can say to his father is, 'Dad, I love you very much. I'm proud of you and I respect you as I do no other.'"

It was then that John asked everyone to stand up and give someone around them a hug. It had come to be one as his father's trademarks. Many there had experienced one. "Look at this as my father's last hug," he finished. I saw Pastor Jacobson's wife coming toward me, and we embraced just when the cameras were pointed in our direction. Thus the phone call when I got home.

David Seering, who'd done some charity TV work with Nitschke over the years, sang a solo called° "In This Very Room." Pastor Jacobson gave the message. It was "The Ray Nitschke Story," one that you'll learn has a happy ending...a very happy ending. It's the story of a man who was angry and mean; he carried it to the field. Then, God gave him his wife Jackie. She became ill and died. Ultimately, that's what saved Ray's very soul. How and why? It's coming up in "The Last Chapter."

The final aspect of the service was the most touching part for me. The honor guard brought the displayed flag and presented it to the family. A tremendous reverence fell over the place at that moment which I can't explain. I don't know why, but it deeply moved us all. It was a fitting conclusion to the service.

Bart Starr hugged each of the Nitschke children and whispered words of love and comfort to each before he left.   I, too, extended my sympathies and requested their blessing to be permitted to include a chapter of the funeral in this book. They graciously consented, and the Lord made a way for it to happen.

Before departing, I had a chance to talk with Reggie. "How's your back, big man?"   He just nodded. I walked away knowing Reggie's retirement was imminent. (Well, I was half right!) I chatted with Sara about their return from a trip to the "Holy Land" just days earlier. As I walked away, I heard Reggie telling a TV reporter that Ray would gently slap his cheek as he talked to him. I caught a conversation in which Brian Noble was telling someone that former Packer Ken Bowman's son had been killed on the way to the funeral.

As I walked out of the church that day, I knew I'd been a part of history in eternity. I really shudder at the thought that I might not have gone. But there are no "what ifs" in God's economy. He had used Chuck to remind me and push me. I believe that the Kingdom of God wouldn't be the same if Ray had not died when he did. Even that was in God's timing, like these words for you.

I am humbled and in awe of the gift of writing this book which God has given me. It has been a blessing to share His words in all three books. Thank you for spending a few hours over the last couple years with me. The pleasure has been mine and the glory is God's.

By design, a hole has been left in this chapter you are reading. My brother in Christ, Arni Jacobson, has agreed to fill in for "The Last Chapter of #66." This chapter could very well fill your God-sized hole and make you whole. The chapter is far too important for me to write and, quite honestly, it is outside of my calling. God has appointed and anointed Pastor Arni for it and he gladly accepted the invitation.

Stay put. Don't stop reading now. You are about to read "the good news," which will bring God to life and make Him real for you. Your eternal life may depend on it!! What you are about to experience is just one page and the last leap of faith away.

CHAPTER 21

The Last Chapter of #66

by Arni Jacobson

On a Sunday morning in 1994, I met the very warm and loving Jackie Nitschke. She had recommitted her life to Jesus Christ and had made Bayside her church home. I asked about her husband, Ray.

"The golf course is his church on Sunday mornings." She always stressed, nonetheless, what an incredibly caring and loving husband and father he was.

Shortly after meeting Jackie, the Nitschkes invited my wife and me to a private box for a Packer game. Ray was very friendly and gracious, but it quickly became obvious that any conversation about God or church would have been quite uncomfortable for him. I discovered later that Ray had struggled in accepting the Lord because he was angry with God for his difficult childhood.

Ray lost his dad, Robert Nitschke, in a car/trolley accident in 1940 when Ray was only three years old. Ten years later, Ray lost his mother, Anna, who was only 41 at the time. By the age of thirteen, Ray was an orphan sent to live with his brother, Richard. Confused, hurt and alone, he asked, "Why did God have to take my mother?" " Why did this have to happen to me?"

Ray admitted, "Without a father, I had less discipline than most boys. And then I lost my mother." It was more than he could handle, and he struggled over the years with any notion of a loving God as a result. Ray also acknowledged that the football field in Green Bay became the place he could take out much of his anger. God did not seem real to Ray, but that would all change on a fall Sunday in 1995.

Jackie had battled cancer over the years. At one point, Ray's daughter Amy called to tell me that Jackie's condition was extremely serious. Pastor Dick Bernal, from San Jose, California, was in town visiting. We went to the hospital where the family had gathered. As Jackie lay in a semi-conscious state, Dick and I laid hands on her and prayed.

Jackie regained consciousness, and with a gleam on her face that defied description, she acknowledged our presence there. But perhaps it was another Presence she was acknowledging for, in that moment, Ray also felt God's presence and the God he had struggled with and kept at a distance for so many years had suddenly become real.

Jackie was released from the hospital just days later. On Saturday, I dropped by to visit and pray with her. Ray followed me out of the room later, and into the hallway. I will never forget that moment. He grabbled me by the shoulders, pulled me to himself, hugged me, and kissed me on the cheek! As he released me, he said, "You're real, and I'm gonna come to your church." The reality that Ray experienced in me that day was the love of Jesus Christ.

Jackie was too ill to come to church that Sunday, but Raymond came. It was then that all of the unanswered questions of his life found the Answer. That morning, at the altar, Ray made a personal profession of faith in Jesus Christ as his Lord and Savior. Soon even his former teammates and golfing buddies were commenting that Ray was in church on Sunday morning, "teeing off" with Jesus at Bayside.

Ray Nitschke was a man who went about doing good. He was always ready to help someone, always giving and generous. As rough as he could be on the field, he would also be the first one to help a lady cross the street in a rainstorm. He had goodness written all over him, and there was a gentleness about him that not many got to see.

It has been both a joy and a blessing to have been Ray Nitschke's pastor. On March 8, God called Ray home to be with Him. When Jackie went to be with the Lord in July of 1996, there was a part of Ray that went with her. Heaven was on Ray's mind since Jackie's departure; he was ready to meet his Master. Ray became a great friend and I loved him dearly. He showed me through his actions that he loved me, too.

Normally, when the Packers played in Green Bay, Ray would come to the early service rather than to the second one so he wouldn't miss the kickoff. Often after the service, he would come to me, reach into his pocket with that big hand, and pull out a ticket. With a gruff voice he'd say, "Here, Pastor, meet me at the game."

When the church service was over, I'd go to Lambeau and virtually run to get into the stadium. Now, suppose I didn't take the ticket out of my pocket. What if I said to the ticket taker, "I'm here to meet Ray Nitschke. Can I get in?" What do you suppose he'd say?

"No way!"

Suppose I pleaded with him. "But, I'm a big Packer fan. Please?"

"No way!"

Until I handed him a ticket, he simply would not let me in. Once I showed him my ticket, however, and he validated it, I would then have free access to the stadium and whoever I was there to meet.

Let me give you an analogy. When Ray Nitschke prayed that simple prayer of faith in Christ, Father God reached down to Ray and handed him a ticket. It was signed in the blood of His Son Jesus. On March 8, 1998, Ray presented that ticket and God the Father validated it. Ray didn't get into God's Hall of Faith because he was a good father or the greatest linebacker to ever play the game of football. He didn't get in there because he signed autographs for anyone who asked.

Ray Nitschke is in the Hall of Faith because he had a "validated ticket" through a personal relationship with Jesus Christ. Death may have ended Ray's life here on earth, but Ray was ushered into the presence of the Lord to begin a new life with Him for all eternity.

I believe God is honoring the commitment made to Him from all the born-again Packers. His hand is on this team. For those players in the Hall of Faith, however, the only thing that is going to matter ultimately is that they have accepted Christ as a personal Savior.

I'd like to ask you the most important question you will ever be asked. If you were to die today, would you have eternal life in heaven because of a personal relationship with Jesus Christ? I'm not asking if you're a member of a specific denomination, or if you go to church every Sunday. Friend, that won't get you into heaven.

Before you close this book, take a moment to look inside your heart. Be honest with yourself. Be honest with God. Ray would want you to do that. If you haven't dealt with the issue of your eternal future, what better time is there than right now?

Ray told me, "Pastor, one thing I like about you is you don't beat around the bush. You go right to the heart of the issue." After his salvation experience, he got right to the heart of the issue, as well.

"Pastor, if you ever do my funeral, I want you to tell people what happened to me. Tell them about Jesus."

That's why I ask you these question. "Are you ready?" "Are you assured of your eternal destiny if you were to die today?"

If you want certainty about your eternal life, and a peace that will sustain you through this life here on earth, I encourage you to pray this prayer now. Don't hesitate. It will be the greatest decision you have ever made for yourself.

> *Dear Jesus,*
> *I am a sinner. And I ask you to come into my life and forgive me of my sins. And Lord, from this day forward I want to serve you. I come to you, the very same God that handed Ray a ticket, and ask you to inscribe one for me right now. I now accept it through the shed blood of Jesus Christ at Calvary. In His name I pray,*
> *Amen.*

Where do you go from here? We would love to help you on this new and exciting journey. Call us at (800) 236-1549.
Thanks for taking the greatest leap of faith!

This Certificate is to Recognize
My Induction into
God's Hall of Faith

By virtue of accepting Jesus Christ as Savior and Lord, I,

_____

(name)

humbly take my place in God's book of life on this _____

(date)

day of _____, _____.

(month)   *(year)*

Keep this book and page near to you or for an
official Hall of Faith certificate with your name inscribed,
send your name, address and phone and date of your induction to:

The Hall of Faith
Box 404, Neenah, WI 54957-0404
e.mail leap@lofrose.com

Your certificate will be mailed out as our gift free of charge.
(Allow 4-6 weeks for delivery)

Pastor Arni Jacobson

For over twenty years, Pastor Arni Jacobson's life and ministry have been dedicated to drawing people to a deeper commitment in worship of and devotion to Jesus Christ. This veteran pastor, community leader, and family man lives his belief that the Christian commitment impacts every part of peoples' lives.

Pastor Jacobson, Sr. Pastor at Bayside Christian Fellowship, is recognized as a soul winner in both his personal life and his pulpit ministry. He has just completed a new book, <u>The Great Omission: Eight Reasons Christians Don't Share Their Faith</u>. His vision is for life-changing growth in peoples' lives and in the kingdom of God; his heartcry is that people would discover Christ through the power of worship, the Word of God, and the works of the Holy Spirit.

RESOURCES

Rawhide Boys Ranch
John and Jan Gillespie, founders
Rawhide Road
New London, WI 54961
920-982-6100

Kathi Pollard, Author/Speaker
WSN Publishing
Box 404
Neenah, WI 54957-0404
920-995-2395

For a TV or radio station affiliate list,
write or call:
Winners Success Radio Network
Box 404
Neenah, WI 54957-0404
920-995-2395

Pastor Arni Jacobson
Bayside Christian Fellowship
3475 Humboldt Rd.
Green Bay, WI. 54311
920-468-1122